CREATIVE PRAYER

Brigid E. Herman

EDITED BY HAL M. HELMS

PARACLETE PRESS
BREWSTER, MASSACHUSETTS

Library of Congress Cataloging-in-Publication Data

Herman, E. (Emily), 1876–1923.
    Creative prayer / by Brigid E. Herman ; edited by Hal M. Helms.
        p.   cm.
    ISBN 1-55725-198-3 (pbk.)
    1. Prayer—Christianity.   I. Helms, Hal McElwaine. II. Title.
BV215.H5   1998
248.3'2—dc21   98-10845
                                                                       CIP

10 9 8 7 6 5 4 3 2 1

© 1998 by The Community of Jesus, Inc.
ISBN: 1-55725-198-3

Published by Paraclete Press
Brewster, Massachusetts
www.paraclete-press.com

Printed in the United States of America.

Editor's Introduction

For many years an abridged version of this book, published by Forward Movement Publications, stood on my bookshelf. Some months ago, I looked at it seeking something on the idea of silence and waiting for God. I was so struck by the clarity and power of what Brigid Herman was saying that I began to explore other parts of this work, and the more I read, the more I liked it.

The book impressed me as saying something vital about the whole subject of prayer, and saying it in a new and fresh way, even though the book was originally written in Britain right after World War I.

I decided to go back to the original edition, and liked what I found there. In a few cases I updated some words and clarified some references, as well as changing a small number of expressions that might lend themselves to misinterpretation in our time.

At this point in the world's history, with problems that continue to bring suffering between peoples and nations generation after generation, can any power equal that of prayer? If indeed prayer is a "creative force," is it not time that people of faith begin to use it in harmony with God's greater will for this world?

Creative Prayer is a ringing challenge to us all to re-think what prayer is, what it does, and how we can become more faithful pray-ers.

Hal M. Helms

Author's Preface

Books on prayer may be roughly divided into those which treat of its scientific aspect, whether from the standpoint of philosophy or from that of psychology, and those which are written with a purely devotional purpose. In these pages I have endeavored to elucidate the meaning and value of prayer as a creative process, whereby the person who prays and his world are made anew.

In Chapter One I have sought to present what I conceive to be the fundamental conditions of prayer as creative energy. "The worshiper," as Professor W. E. Hocking puts it, "does not merely sustain, but creates. All beauty, as Plato thought, incites to reproduction. It incites perhaps to something more than reproduction—to origination. Some superabundance there is in the vision of God which sends the seer back not to the old but to the new." This creative vision is a central element in Christian prayer.

In Chapters Two and Three I have dealt with two great aids to creative prayer—silence and meditation—trying to show that, far from being the esoteric hobbies of mystical devotees, they are essential to the virile discipline of the spiritual life.

Prayer, however, is something more than vision; and if we define it purely in terms of vision, we are in danger of making the mistake of those who imagine that they are on the right path because they happen to see the goal. With this danger in view, I have in Chapter Four endeavored to expound creative prayer as the soul's pilgrimage from self to God. True prayer is our loving response to the love of God; and since Divine Love expressed itself in a supreme act of self-giving, nothing short of a generous and unreserved act of self-giving on our part can constitute a worthy response.

Prayer is not a spiritual romance or a psychic dream, but an act of devotion influencing the very depth of the soul, permeating the whole life and shaping every action. And since this self-surrender is not an isolated act, but involves a habitual and progressive discipline, a lifelong "conversion" from love of self to love of God, I have in Chapter Five set forth the way of self-denial as the path of power. In doing so, I have treated of the ascetic element in the spiritual life, not as a stoic discipline or a joyless self-immolation, but as a genuine and inevitable movement of love—the soul's joyous self-identification with him who for humanity became incarnate and "emptied himself of all but love."

In Chapters Six and Seven I have sought to elucidate the corporate aspect of individual prayer—an aspect often ignored by writers on corporate worship. Creative prayer is both an apostolate and a priesthood. The worshiper, lovingly identified with the redemptive purpose of God, is no longer a self-centered individual, but a priestly member of the Body of Christ. "Through him dumb souls are eloquent"; in him Christ is pierced with the world's sin. Wherever such a one lifts up his lonely soul to God, there is the church and the gospel, the altar and the sacrifice.

My warmest thanks are due to my husband, who has both read the manuscript and revised the proofs, and from whose valuable criticisms and suggestions I have derived much help.

E.H., London

Table of Contents

CHAPTER ONE

The Mystery of Prayer

A RADIANT YOUNG GIRL, the daughter of a wealthy silk merchant of Lyons, was dancing at a fashionable ball. Her gown was the richest, her face the loveliest, and her step the lightest in all that lively assembly. She was engaged to the most popular young man in her social set, and the wedding was due within a week.

Suddenly, in the middle of a minuet, her foot faltered and her eyes grew wide and misty, as she looked past her partner into what had become to her a dull blur of muted colors. A vision had come to her, suddenly, unaccountably, wiping out the festive scene and fixing her eyes upon Eternity.

She, the careless butterfly of only a moment ago, had seen the vision of a dying world. In that flash of unearthly intuition, she knew, with the unshakable certainty of the soul that has been touched by God, that the world was dying for lack of prayer. The world was perishing for lack of vital air. It was cut off from the very source of life, slowly dying the death of the asphyxiated. She seemed to hear its labored breathing—uneven, gasping, spasmodic. She saw creation sink into nothingness and no one there to save, no one even to recognize the peril. Around her, her friends were dancing, unaware that it was a dance of death. In a corner a smiling, debonair priest discussed the relative merits of eligible young men with a matchmaking mother. Ah, what chance for a dying world when the church herself is drugged in slumber!

But God was watching, and in his inscrutable mercy he had awakened her. Why? Why did she stand there, the only watcher among sleepwalkers? With a swift, resolute motion of soul, intense as leaping flame, she then and there renounced all that life had to offer her and vowed herself to ceaseless prayer on behalf of a dying world.

Deaf to the entreaties of parents and lover, impregnable with the strength of those who have *seen*, she entered a convent and became the pioneer of one of the great contemplative orders, the influence of which has gone far beyond the bounds of the Catholic church, and from which the greatest of Christian mystics and reformers have always sprung.

I

PRAYER: THE EXPRESSION OF LIFE

The nun of Lyons does not stand alone in her testimony. Through all the centuries men and women have been awakened to see that the world—yes, and the church also—was dying for lack of prayer. Always and everywhere apostles of prayer have arisen, calling upon a materialized church to cease from the busyness of merely institutional activities and to give herself to the true business of prayer. At every great crisis in the world's history multitudes have rediscovered the secret of prayer, and a tidal wave of petition and intercession has swept through Christendom. But again and again, once the crisis was past and the tension slackened, the voice of prayer became faint and inarticulate, and soon there was only a thin trickle where once the flood had been.

Today we have once more become acutely conscious of the need for prayer. Corporate prayer movements are finding a ready response, and books on prayer are eagerly read. On every hand there is a new interest in the phenomena of the prayer life. And yet it is doubtful if there is actually more prayer in the church—let alone in the world—today than there was in the smooth, complacent days before the World War. There is much curiosity about prayer, and particularly about its psychology; much speculation as to its results, especially in cases of physical and mental disease. But there is no indication that the investigation of prayer has led to serious, sustained, concentrated practice.

Why is this so? No single answer can be given to the question; human nature is too complex a thing to allow an explanation that covers all the facts. One thing that readily suggests itself is that many people who begin with a serious concern about prayer are soon turned away from the main issue by reading a multitude of books on prayer, and are deluded into imagining that they have grasped the reality of prayer because they have gained a superficial acquaintance with the various theories and methods of prayer. Another consideration, grim but unfortunately true, is that for every nine modern Christians who take an interest in institutional work or church finance, scarcely one will respond to a challenge to prayer. To put it bluntly, for the average person of today, the term "spiritual" is unpractical, if not illusory.

But there is one reason for the dearth of prayer of which we have taken all too little account. Throughout the church there are sincere, earnest, thoughtful people, sensitive to the finest issues and honestly striving to serve God, who look upon much praying—and especially upon meetings for corporate prayer—with undisguised suspicion, as based upon a crude and childish conception of God, and as consisting of little more than opportunities for emotional display.

What does this mean? Simply that for generations we have, to all practical intents and purposes, regarded prayer, in a deplorably mechanical way, as a process of unrelenting pleading and begging. I am not referring to our deliberate *theories* of prayer—the best mind of the church in all ages has held a noble theory of prayer—but to our *practice*. As a matter of fact, we have proceeded as if prayer consisted in asking for various temporal and spiritual blessings with reiterative intensity, implying that, provided we asked earnestly enough and persistently enough, God would surely respond to our cry.

Preaching has kept pace with our enlarging thought of God, but there has been comparatively little direct teaching on prayer in the light of that larger conception, and that small amount has been far too theoretical. As a consequence, to hundreds of men and women who have outgrown the traditional conception of God, prayer has become either a merely pious sentiment or an outworn superstition. We suffer, in fact, from arrested development in prayer. Prayer is one of those things we take for granted, very much after the manner of William Law's Mundanus:

> Mundanus[1] is a man of excellent parts and clear apprehension. He is well advanced in age and has made a great figure in business. Every part of trade and business that has fallen in his way has had some improvement from him, and he is always contriving to carry any method of doing anything well to its greatest height. . . . The only thing which has not fallen

[1] Mundanus: (Latin) the man of the world.

under his improvement, nor received any benefit from his judicious mind, is his devotion. This is in just the same poor state as it was when he was only six years of age, and the old man prays now in that little form of words which his mother used to hear him repeat night and morning. . . . If Mundanus sees a book of devotion, he passes it by as he would a spelling book, because he remembers that he learned to pray at his mother's knee.

Mundanus still lives among us, and may be found in quantity in every Christian congregation. In his secular affairs he often shows a marked, and not always quite pleasant, astuteness; in his commerce with God he is positively childish—in everything except the childlike heart, without which we cannot enter the Kingdom of God. For his conception of God—if indeed an inherited convention can be called a conception—is scarcely adequate to the intelligence of a thoughtful schoolchild.

II

CONVERSATION WITH GOD

"Lord, teach us to pray!" pleaded the disciples. And our Lord gave them a norm of prayer which has nourished the faith and life of the church of all ages, produced a science of prayer which is still in its infancy, and given exhaustless treasures of thought to the noblest minds. We of today, however, tend to deny that prayer can be taught in any sense. We insist upon its lyrical spontaneity. It is "the soul's sincere desire, uttered or unexpressed"—as natural as the cry of the newborn babe or the groan of the dying. It is, indeed, of the essence of genius: who can produce genius by dint of hard work?

This is one of the fallacies peculiar to the religious mind. In all other realms of human thought or activity, genius, far from being regarded as a dispensation from rigid discipline, is looked upon as the only sufficient justification for the highest form of training. And in the case of so vital an achievement as prayer the discipline must be correspondingly thorough. It is not by merely forming study circles, or reading books on prayer, that we enter into its mysteries and know its power, but by a discipline *co-extensive with life itself*. Prayer is, in the last resort, worth exactly as much—or as little—as the person behind it. If those who pray have an obstinate, prejudiced, undisciplined mind, their prayer will suffer from the same defects. If their desires are limited, gross, and ill-guided, so will their prayer be.

This does not mean, of course, that we can afford to wait to begin to pray until we have secured the ideal presuppositions (we may as well try to learn to swim on a table!), but simply that we must bear in mind from first to last that *prayer is the expression of a life*.

Prayer is not the whole of the spiritual life, or even, taken by itself, the most important factor in it. It rises out of an environment which determines its quality. While the faithful practice of prayer cannot fail to react upon the personality, we cannot achieve true personality simply by praying for certain virtues. It is here that the average adult fails to transcend the notions of childhood. We still have a vague but persistent idea that all we need do is simply to pray to be "made good." We may clothe that idea in quite ambitious language, but in its essence it is the same that possessed us when we were little children at our mother's knee; and the same sense of disappointment still overtakes us when, in some quiet moment, we realize that, with all our praying to be made wise and patient and upright, we are not really any richer in these qualities than we were before. We are slow to learn that effective prayer involves a constant interaction between the quality of soul we bring to our prayers and the sincerity of our desire. To pray to be made wise is the merest superstition, unless we bring to our prayer the kind of soul that is capable of acquiring wisdom. We are responsible not only for our prayers, but for providing the background against which prayer can energize. It is not too much, indeed, to say that for every thought we give to prayer itself—excepting, of course, the actual practice of prayer, which is vital at every stage—we should give ten to the life behind the prayer.

When we consider the fundamental nature of prayer, the importance of this background becomes clearly apparent. We have come to regard prayer very largely as a process by which we are to avail ourselves of the spiritual forces of the universe. Given the firm conviction that we live in a spiritual universe, and that a demand based upon this conviction will be answered, prayer yields sure results. The prayer of faith, we say, is subject to definite, readily ascertainable laws, and once we pray in accordance with these laws, all things are possible to us, for we are "wired with God," yoked with the forces of omnipotent Goodness. We can remove mountains of difficulty which before seemed insuperable, and call into being whole continents of good "out of nothing." We think of Albrecht Bengel stilling a destructive tempest with a prayerful wave of his hand, and of George Muller praying his great orphanage into existence. And we argue that the sole reason why miracles do not follow prayer today is that the wave of materialistic science which is now ebbing away has left a stubborn sediment of fundamental unbelief in the triumph of spirit over matter.

But while this view represents one aspect of prayer which

modern psychology has made particularly attractive, it does not touch the heart of the subject. To know what prayer really is, we must study it from the center. And its central significance is not that of a spiritual process by which mountains are removed and benefits evoked. Prayer in its essence is communion with God. The simplest analogy—that of loving, trustful discourse between friend and friend—is also the most profound.

The conception of prayer as the soul's secret, intimate conversation with God is neglected by many, because it seems to them to make prayer a narrowly individualistic exercise. But we do not argue in this fashion when the intimacies of the family or of friendship are concerned. We find it quite natural and reasonable that the life and influence of even the most altruistic of public persons should be crucially determined by the sacred relationships of home. We are quite ready to admit the fact that a person's home life and friendships have more to do with his work for the world than a whole lifetime of public activity. This is a truism which we never dream of questioning. But we seem curiously reluctant nowadays to believe that the prayer of friendship with God is the most influential type of prayer.

To realize that it is indeed so, one need only read the biographies of those whose lives have been nourished by prayer. Without a single exception, the type of prayer that shaped their lives and overflowed in blessing upon their generation was not so much a deliberate moral and spiritual process—the pressing of the button that releases creative energy, the scientific establishment of contact with the powerhouse of divine, electrifying force—but simple heart-communion with their heavenly Father. To them faith meant primarily not belief in the availability and efficiency of spiritual forces, and in the definiteness and uniformity of the laws that govern them, but personal trust, deepening from year to year with their deepening intimacy with God.

Once we grasp this, we will realize that the condition of this prayer of communion is a right attitude of soul. As in human love and friendship, it is not moral perfection that is required. The most broken soul may enter that magic realm. Who ever loved or was loved on account of mere moral excellence? Yet the soul that would know the secret of friendship must possess very definite moral and spiritual characteristics. It must be purged of prejudice and prepossession, and it must have a single eye towards the beloved. A person who approaches a friend chock-full of his own opinions and concerns, looking upon the friend only as affording welcome opportunity for self-expression, will never get beyond the outer court of the temple. Nor will one who is encumbered with a thousand rival occupations and interests ever learn to spell the name of the friend correctly.

III

PRAYER: GROUNDED IN GOD'S LOVE

Thus we are met, on the very threshold of prayer, by a moral demand. Friendship with God presupposes the beginnings of genuine humility and of fundamental simplicity of purpose. Without humility—that is, without reality—there can be no power in prayer; and without singleness, no love.

We all tend to be infatuated with the idea of strength—that is why definitions of prayer in terms of "force" appeal to us so strongly—but we fail to realize that all true strength is grounded in humility. We still relegate humility to the pale ranks of passive virtues and ornamental graces, whereas in its legitimate development it is a stout and soldierly quality. Indeed, humility is simply a sense of reality and proportion. It is grounded upon a knowledge of the truth about ourselves and about God. "The reason God is so great a lover of humility," says St. Vincent de Paul, with his characteristic forthrightness, "is that he is the great lover of truth. Now humility is nothing but truth, while pride is nothing but lying."

The same testimony was borne by Sister Thérèse of Lisieux when, as she lay dying, one of the nuns praised her for her humility. "Yes," she assented, without a trace of that self-depreciation which is a form of inverted pride, "for it has always seemed to me that humility is simply truth. I do not know whether I am humble, but I do know that my soul has ever sought the truth. Yes, I have understood humility of heart."

Humility stands for perfect soundness of mind. It represents the life that is ranged round its rational center. It means that the soul has found its level in the world of reality. Every person who finds his center in self is on the way to madness—is, indeed, already a little mad. When Peer Gynt found himself in the lunatic asylum, he could not realize that the people around him were mad. They talked so sensibly and well, they discussed their affairs and plans with such lucidity and shrewdness that he was amazed. He turned to the physician-in-charge for enlightenment. "Ah," said the doctor, "don't you see how it is? They talk very sensibly, I admit, but it's all about themselves. They are, in fact, most intelligently obsessed with self. It's all self—morning, noon, and night. We can't get away from self here. We lug it along with us, even through our dreams. Oh, yes, young sir, we talk sensibly; but we're mad right enough, all the same."

At least one-half of what we miscall humility, especially the habit of self-accusation and self-abasement that passes for a deep sense of sin, is the fruit of self-obsession. The chronic depression and despondency that go along with a certain type of religious temperament are simply the outcome of lacerated pride. We are disappointed with ourselves, not because we are humble, but, quite on the contrary, because we thought too highly of ourselves and are wounded in our pride. As St. Francis de Sales put it, "We are angry because we have been angry; impatient at having shown impatience." Pride is known most surely not by its swagger, but by its quickness to grow bitter and despondent. The soul that is truly humble takes its faults quietly, and goes on afresh in confidence and hope. For humility rests not upon self-contemplation, but upon a vision of God.

To approach God in prayer with humility is "to know what it means to be a created being, and to have a Creator." That seems the most elementary of truisms, but it includes the whole philosophy of prayer. To come to God as the fountain of our being, the inspirer of our prayers, the great sustainer without whose upholding arm we must sink back into nothingness—how far removed such an attitude is from that in which we habitually draw near to him! Our prayers are blighted by self-consciousness. When we are not paralyzed by doubt, we are preoccupied with the recital of our woes and wrongs, our aspirations and ambitions. We tend to forget that in God we live and move and have our being, and we approach him as if we had come to reason and plead with one like unto ourselves, "only bigger." And when we are reminded that the truth is far other, that prayer is as the returning of waters to the spring from which they went forth, the offering up of a sacrifice which is, like that of Abraham, "of the Lord's providing," we retort that all this belongs to the old, superseded view of God as an oriental despot with absolute rights over his subjects.

But is there not something akin to this humble sense of dependence in the highest human friendship? Is not love a sacrament that must be taken kneeling? We come to the Friend of our heart, and as we open our soul to him we realize that it is of his own that we are giving him. That impulse of love, that worthy aspiration, that new outlook upon life— it is of his creating. As we are initiated into the mystery of friendship, we know that our friend is not merely "another"; he speaks to us not from without, but from the center of our being. He is in us and we in him. His influence is profoundly mystical; no merely temperamental affinity can account for friendship at its highest potency. Deep down in the abysmal mystery of being the thread was spun that linked soul to soul. My Friend creates me and recreates me. In him I come to know my true self. His love and trust purge me of sin by shame and contrition; his gentleness makes me great; his high expectations make all things possible to me. And what is true in a limited measure of human friendship is wholly true of humanity's communion with its Creator, *for the very act of creation is nothing else than the outgoing of infinite Love.*

God loved us into being, and in acknowledging him as our maker we open our inmost nature to the Friend whose love is creative power and whose might is self-emptying love. Ever since we were born his creative and sustaining influence was upon us, and in the prayer of humility we consciously open our hearts to the power that worked there from our earliest days without our conscious concurrence. We welcome the love that has access to the most secret springs of our being, and we lay our secrets bare to the sympathy that knows us as we can never know ourselves. Knowing God as "the master-light of all our seeing," we know ourselves to be blind. Glimpsing the beauty of his holiness, we see ourselves stained and polluted. Hearing the voice of self-giving love, the shame and misery of our soul cry out for redemption. Bowing in awe and penitence before the almighty Judge, we know the secret of supreme friendship. Such is the great paradox of Christian prayer. And the heart that desires the supreme friendship must be undivided in its aim. The grace of prayer is the grace of the single eye.

When we read the lives of the saints, we are struck by a certain large leisure which went hand in hand with a remarkable effectiveness. They were never hurried; they did comparatively few things, and these not necessarily striking or important; and they troubled very little about their influence. Yet they always seemed to hit the mark; their simplest actions had a distinction, an exquisiteness that suggested the artist. The reason is not hard to find. Their sainthood lay in their habit of referring the smallest actions to God. They lived in God; they acted from a pure motive of love towards God. They were as free from self-regard as from slavery to the good opinion of others. God saw and God rewarded: what else did they need? They possessed God and possessed themselves in God. Hence the inalienable dignity of these meek, quiet figures who seem to produce such marvelous effects with such humble materials.

But we of today scarcely ever possess ourselves. Our hearts are ceaselessly vexed with a mixed multitude of imaginings and aims. We belong to the movements and causes we are interested in, whereas it is they that would belong to us, if we were indeed Christ's, as Christ is God's. We no longer wait upon God at every turn; we are too hurried and distracted for such waiting. Our self-imposed duties tread on each other's heels, and when at last we compose ourselves for our final rest, we are conscious that, with all our doing, we have accomplished very little. For we lack that guarded heart, that grace of priestly discretion, which says, "I hold myself for God; I hold all other things in and for the sake of God."

To say God, and mean the world; to name Christ, and

intend self—what state could be more deplorable? And so long as we come to prayer distracted by a multitude of interests which we have never yet brought to the light of God's countenance, weighed down by a thousand and one occupations concerning which we have never yet sought the will of God, we shall still be seeking ourselves, no matter how urgently we address God. Friendship implies a heart at leisure from itself. The supreme friendship demands a singleness of devotion, a simplicity and perfection of "intention towards God," which spells liberty and power. It is purity of intention we need—the direction of our whole nature towards God. Where that intention is not only present but pure, steadfast, and consistently loving, God's creative energy flows into the spirit. The whole life is re-ordered after a divine pattern, and henceforth bears the seal of a supernatural distinction.

We know how an absorbing devotion to a great ideal or, more potently still, to a beloved person, simplifies and unifies life. And to the soul that is wholly bent upon God, the thousand fretting cares and vexing problems that tear the lives of others in pieces simply cease to exist. With the submerging of the irrelevant, the soul is free to give itself to that which really matters. Life becomes henceforth triumphantly effective. It is no more the happy hunting-ground of vagrant impulses and futile efforts; it is the theater of divine activity, the sphere of creative power. Its circumference is governed from the center.

IV

THE PRAYER THAT MOVES MOUNTAINS

It does not matter how we approach the subject, provided we come to real grips with it. Sooner or later we shall see that the many questions and difficulties that gather round the prayer life may be reduced to the one momentous question of our relationship to him with whom we desire to hold communion. What about our relation to God? That is the question which we are inclined to shirk, but which mercifully refuses to be silenced. It persists through all philosophical evasions and theological hair-splitting, through all intellectual doubts and moral problems. There are many valid difficulties about prayer, and we must face them; but in grappling with them we shall come to see that they are not fundamental, and that their solution depends upon our attitude towards a deeper problem.

Let us put it quite plainly. The real question at issue is whether we have the kind of relation to God that is the only basis of prayer at its highest and best. We are not dealing here with the universal human need of prayer. No one can doubt for a moment that the cry wrung from a soul in bitter need and anguish—the prayer of parents for their dying children, the pleading of those that gather round sickbeds, the inarticulate outcry of a soul suddenly face to face with its sin—is genuine prayer and swiftly reaches the heart of God. What we are concerned with is Christian prayer in its full potency—the prayer of faith that removes mountains, the prayer of intercession that stands between a people and their punishment till the plague is stayed, the prayer that makes the saint and the seer, that high commerce with God which is concentrated creative power.

As we consider prayer at the level at which it becomes a

channel of creative power, most of the difficulties which surround its more elementary aspects will be resolved. For prayer, like any other human activity, can be judged rightly only by observing its normal manifestations; and it is not the more common forms of prayer, but the rarer ones, that represent the normal. The lower forms—for example, the spasmodic, instinctive cry of need—are instances of arrested development, and it is as unfair to measure prayer by them as to judge the strength of the human body from observing an invalid. Not the frenzied cry of sudden anguish, but the calm, trustful committal of faith, is the normal attitude of the praying soul. Not the answered prayer of the mother whose child is spared, but the apparently unanswered prayer of our Lord in the Garden, is the classic instance.

And in taking prayer at its purest and highest as the starting point of our theory and the goal of our practice, we see that prayer, far from being a tiresomely reiterated asking based upon a conception of God that belongs to the childhood of the race, is the highest and most dynamic form of interaction between the human and the divine. It is the whole personality—intellect as well as emotion and will—energized in fellowship with the Lord of all life. Prayer is humanity consciously apprehending its high destiny and stretching towards it. It is not merely one of the noblest and most fruitful activities of the soul, at once the most intensely individual and the most comprehensively social, but the fount and the consummation of all noble activity.

The fatal habit of contrasting prayer and action is deeply ingrained in the modern mind, and we persist in taking it as a mere figure of speech when we hear prayer defined as a succession of vital acts. The old prejudice against what is called the contemplative state survives, in spite of our modern infatuation with weird theories of "thought-forces" and "psychic currents," and sustained prayer continues to be regarded by the majority of sensible people as suitable only for invalids and others who are debarred from an active life.

But the moment we make an honest attempt to get at the central meaning of unselfish activity, we find that its fundamental significance is identical with that of prayer. What, after all, is the most important function of the active worker, say, in the slums of a great city? It is not merely to relieve poverty, or to lessen the sum of human misery. Indeed, it might be argued that in protracting the lives of the feeble, the diseased, and the generally inefficient, such a worker actually adds to the sum of human misery in helping to perpetuate a defective type.

But the central object and the most potent effect of the worker's activity is, in reality, something quite different. It is positive, not negative. It consists not in alleviating suffering, but in creating an atmosphere in which faith and hope, selfless love and devoted service, health and happiness become not only possible but easy and natural. His pity purges the fetid spiritual atmosphere; his devotion propagates itself and kills the noisome growths of selfishness, as the germs of health overcome the morbid bacilli of disease; his consecrated personality releases imprisoned powers of good in the most unlikely quarters.

As the worker goes about his work, he restores the choked wells of trust and healing in the embittered of the poor, and liberates the tide of brotherhood in the sealed hearts of the rich. He awakens high aspirations in those who live in poverty, and inspires heroic devotion in the children of privilege. Any material improvement or social reform that he may secure is a by-product of this central process of prayer; its excellence depends entirely upon its connection with such a process.

The twentieth century has revealed the essential

sordidness and hopelessness of social progress that does not spring from a heart of religious devotion. We have seen how the brute in humanity thrives under advanced economic, social, and intellectual conditions. It would almost seem that wherever social reform is based upon no sanctions beyond itself, there it becomes the breeding ground of a new race of human apes and tigers, more shapely on the surface but more monstrous within than the old beasts of the slum jungle.

Argue as we may, the saints were right. The central source of all genuinely beneficent activity is prayer. One who "merely" prays, if it be the prayer of communion with God, is more truly a benefactor of the race than a person who endows a foundling hospital; and the time will come when the great philanthropies will be traced back to their source in the prayers of humble, obscure folk whom the world agreed to despise. Nothing good can ever come to humankind except by our union with the creative energy of God—a union that is unconsciously present wherever a soul is on fire with love and compassion, and that is consciously realized in the prayer of communion.

Father Baker was right when he averred that the external well-being of the nation as well as of the church depended more largely than we imagine upon hidden persons of prayer. "Those inexpressible devotions which they exercise, and in which they tacitly involve the needs of the whole church, are far more prevalent with God than the busy endeavors and prayers of ten thousand others. A few such secret and unknown servants of God are the chariots and horsemen, the strength and bulwarks, of the kingdoms and churches where they live."[2]

Such prayer—prayer that changes both those who pray

---

[2] *Sancta Sophia*, p. 508.

and the world they live in—is not achieved without concentrated effort. It demands a committal of soul, a self-surrender, which takes us into the deepest heart of religion. To make this surrender is to become a high priest of divine mysteries. But while there are those who in a flash, as it were, pass from the marketplace to the Holy of Holies, most souls need to traverse the outer court and to tarry in the place of preparation. Two trusty aids await us there: silence and meditation. Quasi-occult writers have so represented both as to prejudice us against them. But, as we shall see, they are not mysterious and fanciful pursuits, peculiar to the high-strung devotees of mystical cults. They are, on the contrary, part of the natural discipline of the healthy soul bent upon communion with God. They are as simple as daylight and as sensible as reason itself.

CHAPTER TWO

The Ministry of Silence

WE HAVE BEEN ACCUSTOMED to regard the cultivation of silence as part of an esoteric mechanism, or, if we believe it to be a genuine spiritual discipline, as exclusively connected with contemplative prayer. We look upon it as a counsel of perfection for persons of much leisure and of a meditative turn of mind, who aspire to those high forms of prayer which seem to us dangerously akin to trance experiences and other psychic phenomena.

What we need to learn is that the practice of silence is sound wisdom for common folk bent upon the prayer of intimate communion; that, indeed, it is the preliminary discipline *par excellence* for all who wish to enter the great world of prayer. The sense of unreality that so insistently haunts the beginner in prayer is due to the fact that he is engaged in a monologue and not in a conversation. For the object of prayer is not merely to find expression for one's deepest yearnings, but to converse with Another, to hear the divine call, and to feel the divine response to the movement of the soul. And it is as impossible to realize our communion with God without the practice of silence, as it is to conduct a conversation with oneself.

As we approach prayer by the spacious antechamber of silence, we come to realize that the first mover is not we, but God. The prayer that rises to our lips as passionate beseeching of a Father's care and sympathy is not a pleading at our own initiative: it is rather the response to an advance. Its very passion is inspired by the Spirit who broods over the soul's formless waters and brings articulate expression out of a voiceless waste of need. Prayer always begins with God. As the little child learns its first prayers from its mother's lips, the soul learns to pray from God. There is not a half-formed aspiration or a heavenward impulse that was not first "inspoken" into the heart by the Spirit who makes intercession for us. We could not pray aright unless the Lord of Prayer taught us, and the only prayers that remain unanswered are the prayers that he does not inspire.

But we so often refuse to come to prayer through the antechamber of silence. We will not wait and listen for the prayers he is waiting to pray in and through us. The result is a long, weary, discouraging monologue, which grows intolerable as we become aware of our aloneness. None except the vividly imaginative, who delight in weaving romances around themselves, can sustain the monologue indefinitely; after a time, the heart grows sick with hope deferred, and we abandon prayer as a dreary form of self-soliloquy—like a make-believe talking through a telephone with no one listening at the other end.

Yet, if we only knew it, a resort to attentive silence would make even these self-willed prayers alive with the reality of the divine response. The Spirit whom we disregarded in the framing of our prayers is waiting to guide them still, clarifying our vision, deepening our insight, taking the hidden treasure of Christ and showing it to our beclouded eyes. When prayer seems a hallucination, the simple expedient of hushing the soul to silence often serves to assure us, beyond all doubting, of the reality of our contact with the Unseen. It is upon our willingness to listen and hear God speak that our prayer life from first to last depends. This should be clear when we remember that prayer is the soul's pilgrimage from self to God; and the most effectual remedy for self-love and self-absorption is the habit of humble listening.

I

SILENCE: THE MASTER-KEY

Thoughtful people everywhere are awake to the therapeutic and recreative force of silence. It is the wisdom of the wanderer who, wearied and sore at heart, comes home at dusk and is stabbed by his sense of strangeness amid the familiar surroundings of his own country. In a passage of luminous quality, Mr. George "A. E." Russell has voiced this wisdom. It records the mood of one who, after a year's sojourn in the sordid city, comes back to the green land he loves:

> I felt like a child who wickedly stays from home through a long day, and who returns frightened and penitent at nightfall, wondering whether it will be received with forgiveness by its mother. Would the Mother of us all receive me again as one of her children? Would the winds with wandering voices be as before the evangelists of her love? . . . I knew if benediction came how it would come. I would sit among the rocks with shut eyes, waiting humble as one waits in the antechambers of the mighty, and if the invisible ones chose me as companion they would begin with a soft breathing of their intimacies creeping on

me with shadowy affection like children who steal nigh to the bowed head and suddenly whisper fondness on the ear before it has even heard a footfall. So I stole out of the cottage and over the dark ridges to the place of rocks, and sat down and let the coolness of the night chill and still the fiery dust in the brain. I waited trembling for the faintest touch, the shyest breathings of the Everlasting within my soul, the sign of reception and forgiveness. I knew it would come.

We of today have lost the sure-footed certainty that our spiritual fathers had. We do not claim to have attained; we cannot even be said to press towards the mark, for the mark is often hidden from our dull and wavering eyes. But even though the goal looms dim in the mist and we are not quite certain of the way, we stand wistfully waiting for someone or something to set us on the path.

We wait, but lack the wisdom of them that wait. We wait impatiently, feverishly turning the pages of a hundred guide-books, making voluble inquiries of this expert and that, embarking upon any and every adventure that tempts our vagrant fancy. We are even violent at times, but with all our violence we do not take the Kingdom by force.

Then, exhausted with our profitless gropings and flutterings, we listen, perchance, to a stray prophet who reminds us that there is such a thing as a divine science of waiting, and that its master-key is silence—the deep, full stillness of the expectant soul. "Be still, and know that I am God."

But we hesitate. The vogue of pseudo-mysticism, with its jargon about recollection, concentration, and "going into the silence," has prejudiced us against the deliberate cultivation of spiritual stillness. And we also hesitate for another and deeper reason. We know that silence is indeed an unexplored realm, peopled with disquieting apparitions and brimful of unguessed terrors for the chance traveler. Anyone who has honestly tried to still his soul—to wean intellect and will and emotion from their external activity to a concurrent attitude of quiet expectancy—has sensed possibilities of weird experiences, compared to which the most "successful" spiritualistic seance would appear trite and tame.

For we too have sojourned too long in the dusty city of external relationships. We have gazed so fixedly and persistently upon the pageantry of passing things that they have become our only reality. We have lived so deeply in the lives of our neighbors and our community—and in the mere shell of their lives at that—that we have lost track of that mysterious "buried life" of ours which is the only real life we possess. Our very religion has become little more than a vigorous effort to be sociable and communicative. Impulses that should breed resolution in our souls are exhausted in resolutions on paper, and thoughts that should condense to strong purpose evaporate in a moist vapor of small talk. As a result, silence of any kind has become difficult. The moment the noise about us stops, we become disquieted and ill at ease. Accustomed to commune with anyone and everyone, we have lost the art of communing with our own spirits, and the prospect of such self-communing does not inspire us with confidence.

And yet a deep instinctive wisdom—part of our inheritance from an age when souls dwelt alone and walked with God—tells us that in quietness lies our salvation. It has been well said that in darkness the eyes are opened, and in silence the heart speaks. He, too, was a wise man who first discovered that in order to live we must stand aloof from what the crowd calls living; and so was that other unknown scribe who told us that "silent men are kings, for they rule over a great country where none can follow them." And if the stillness of self-communing is a veritable well of life and healing, what of that "silence of the soul that waits for more than man to teach"? Yes, we know ourselves to have been in the far country, and, having returned to our own land, our only wisdom is to close our eyes and wait humbly, "as one waits in the antechambers of the mighty," for the reconciling touch of God.

For, say what we will—and the conviction will not be accepted unchallenged by the mind of today—a discipline of solitude and silence is essential for those who would acquaint themselves with God and be at peace. We are living in an age that has discovered the meaning and value of corporateness. Fellowship is its watchword, and community of experience its aim. And the eye of the age has seen truly, for until the individual knows himself as a member of corporate humanity, his personal experience must remain fragmentary and barren. We are in sober truth members one of another, and it is only in fellowship that we can realize God's purpose.

But where we are continually led astray is in confounding vital corporateness with mere gregariousness, or with sociability and communicativeness, or with outward uniformity of opinion and action. All these may exist apart from any vital fellowship. They are, in fact, not essential to fellowship at all and often constitute its most stubborn hindrance. The solitary worshiper who really touches God, and touches him not with a merely self-regarding motive, but with a heart of love for all humanity and a tender fellow-feeling with human need and woe, is engaged in a more genuine act of fellowship than a thousand gregarious individuals who mistake external togetherness for vital unity. Such a person is worshiping with the whole church catholic, and, like his Lord, seeks to sanctify himself for his brethren's sake. We need not decry togetherness; it is a necessity for the normal human being, and experiences are possible to a company of people of one heart and mind that are not possible for even the noblest and saintliest individual alone. But we constantly tend to take it for granted that mere togetherness is equivalent to true unity, and that the person who feels within himself the divine call to solitude and silence is thereby cutting himself off from the fellowship. Such an assumption is entirely contrary to fact.

It is not without significance that the earliest spirituality of the post-apostolic church ran along the line of solitude and silence. We are repelled, if not positively appalled, by the picture of the Fathers of the Desert drawn with such scrupulous fidelity by Palladius in his book *Paradise*. Their ruthless violence to every natural instinct; their severe, and often grotesque and even disgusting, physical austerities; their narrow outlook and stern piety, all combine to make them particularly unattractive to an age that counts all natural impulses divine.

And yet no impartial reader of these strange lives and collections of remarkable sayings can avoid the conclusion that, however deplorable their eccentricities and excesses, these men were profoundly right in believing that he who wants to be the friend of Christ must forsake much that the world counts friendship; that he who desires to see God must close his eyes to many things that the world thinks desirable; and that he who wishes to hear the voice of the Spirit must stop his ears against the babel of tongues and put a seal upon his lips. Their lives bore irrefutable witness to the truth that was in them. The wisdom that is foolishness to people was never justified more convincingly than in these children of the desert.

For as we read their histories, we realize that there, in the silence of the wilderness, amid the grim exactions of a merciless ideal, the very humanities in whose name we protest against such an ideal came to birth and were fostered. Did a sick or friendless stranger need food, lodging, and careful nursing? It was in the rocky cells of the wilderness he got it. For to the Fathers of the Desert hospitality was a duty that ranked higher than almost any other, and when a stranger came to a hermit's door, the holy man would ply him with the best food at his command, and, in the true spirit of delicate hospitality, break his fast and eat with him. Did a heartbroken sinner, scorned by the world and cast out by the church, seek compassion and tender human sympathy? It was to the solitaries that he turned in his bitter hour, for these austere and silent men had discovered the secret of Christ's love for the outcast, in an age when the church had already forgotten it. Did famine or pestilence scourge the cities? It was to the men of the desert they sent to tend the sick, organize collections, and superintend the distribution of food.

It was these men, whom we like to regard as inhuman and unpractical, that tried to alleviate the misery of prisoners thirteen centuries before Elizabeth Fry sent camels and boats laden with food to the half-starved populations of remote cities. And in an age when tenderness to animals was looked upon as an unpleasant kind of madness, it was these men who anticipated St. Francis in their idyllic relations to the wild beasts and their kindliness towards every living thing.

Robert Louis Stevenson, in his spirited defense of Father Damien, meets the jibes of the priest's critics, who accused him of uncleanly habits, by reminding them that it was this man of doubtful cleanliness who had provided a clean abode for those whom the rest of the world had left in filth and misery. "There was not a pan or a pot on Molokai that dirty Damien had not washed." And so it might be said of the

Fathers of the Desert that there was not a kindly and humane impulse within the Christendom of that day that did not find its pioneer and apostle among the gaunt, "inhuman" ascetics of the wilderness. They turned their backs upon a world that thought them mad and proved their sublime sanity by the fruits they brought from the land of silence and poverty. Charities beside which our modern institutions seem dismal and lifeless; a sense of spiritual values to which we are only now slowly approaching; a brotherliness towards all feeble, needy, broken people, and especially towards womanhood, which the church of today has still to learn—these and many other gifts they bequeathed to the ages to come.

And it has ever been thus. The great silent men, who judged even lawful pleasures inexpedient for Christ's athletes, and voluntarily narrowed their lives and emptied themselves of many things they would jealously have coveted had they not coveted the "one thing" even more jealously—it has always been they who anticipated the world's greatest reforms, inspired it with its noblest ideals, brought loveliness out of the unlovely, and by their poverty made many rich. They were not all ascetics in the conventional sense, but they were all lovers of silence, and not afraid to dwell apart. Doing their work in the world, they made time for quiet brooding, for large and heroic solitude, even though that time had to be stolen from social joys or wrested from sleep.

If we read the biographies of the great and wise, be they statesmen or priests, teachers or poets, Roman Catholics or Quakers, we shall find that they were individuals of long silences and deep ponderings. Whatever of vision, of power, of genius there was in their work was wrought in silence. And when we turn to the inner circle of the spiritual masters—the men and women, not necessarily gifted or distinguished, to whom God was "a living, bright reality" which supernaturalized their everyday life and transmuted their homeliest actions into sublime worship—we find that their roots struck deep into the soil of spiritual silence. Living in the world and rejoicing in sweet human relationships, they yet kept a little cell in their hearts whither they might run to be alone with God.

II
THE SECRET OF SILENCE

We know that this is so. We too have tried to practice this pregnant silence, but the results have been disappointing. Whether we sought help from such corporate movements as the Fellowship of Silence, or tried to hush our souls in solitude, we have found it a difficult and futile experiment. To begin with, we were torn asunder by a thousand and one distractions. Scarcely had we resolved to be silent, when a swarm of intruding thoughts, many of them absurdly irrelevant, laid siege to our souls. Trifles that had not caused us a moment's reflection before, suddenly assumed a morbid importance. Considerations we would have brushed aside under any other circumstances presented themselves again and again with grotesque insistence and we were helpless against them. Business problems and family cares pressed upon us with a weight they never had previously. Then we became acutely conscious of our bodies, which rebelled against the unwonted stillness. Every nerve grew acutely sensitive. The ticking of the clock, the crackling of a log in the grate, the slightest sound or movement became a small torture to the sensitive and tried the temper of the more robust.

And when at last we gained the upper hand over these distractions, one of two things happened. Either our silence degenerated into idle daydreaming or a dull emptiness that left one yawning, or else it sharpened into a state of a futile expectancy. It became dense, strained, uncanny. The tension was that of painful listening, as of one who strains his ear for the sound of a footfall which he knows in his heart will never come. And it all ended in a loss of vitality. One's tone was lowered. After all this expenditure of energy one was left with nothing more substantial than the weakness of a reaction to a purely artificial strain. It was as if a man had clenched his fist and driven it, with all the weight of his muscle, into the empty air.

We have looked for the cause of our failure to achieve the dynamic silence of the saints in every direction but the right one. We have studied various methods and directions, turned in our despair to the fanaticisms of unwise and unhealthy counselors, and wasted time and energy in trying to force ourselves into a mood as artificial as it was momentary. Finally we persuaded ourselves that "times have changed." The brooding silence of the saints in which so many great things were born seems incompatible with a modern background. They lived in days of spiritual leisure, when problems were few and simple, and a dormant social conscience allowed them to concentrate upon the business of "making their souls."

But the truth lies elsewhere. The one fact we forget is that the saints were capable of spiritual silence simply because they had not contracted our modern habit of ceaseless talk in their ordinary life. Their days were days of silence, relieved by periods of conversation, while ours are a wilderness of talk with a rare oasis of silence.

It is useless to imagine that one can pass at a bound from a daily round in which the lust of talk absorbs three-fourths of the soul's energy to a state of harmonious, revealing stillness.

The practice of silence must begin, not in the office and the home, the playing field and the church. The soul whose virility has been allowed to ooze out through the tongue during eleven hours of the day need not hope to regain it during the silent twelfth hour. To put it bluntly, the first step towards attaining interior quiet is to hold one's peace more frequently and to better purpose in the ordinary ways of life. "Silence," says Thomas Carlyle, "is the element in which great things fashion themselves together, that at length they may emerge fully formed and majestic into the daylight of life which they are henceforth to rule. Do thou thyself but hold thy tongue for one day, and on the morrow how much clearer are thy purpose and duties; what wreck and rubbish have the mute workmen within thee swept away when intrusive noises were shut out!"

We have yet to accept and act upon the axiom that the cultivation of a habit of silence is an integral part of all true education, and that children, far from looking upon a demand for silence as an unnatural and intolerable imposition, have an inborn aptitude for quietness. To realize the truth of this, one need only witness the silent time in a Montessori school. The blinds are drawn, the signal is given, and each little head is bowed as a happy stillness, free from any morbid taint, descends upon the children. It is real silence, not lazy half-dozing. No attempt is made to suggest a theme for meditation, and yet something akin to true meditation takes place; for when the teacher's voice calls the children by name, one by one, into the light of the adjoining room, they come as those who have learned a wonderful and happy secret. There is a hint of depth in the merry eyes, a suggestion of more than physical health and peace in their whole bearing. A strange beauty, an elusive freshness as of morning dew, seems to have been added to the natural childish vitality and charm that are so delightful in themselves. Whatever one may think of the Montessori system, few would question the wisdom of that spell of quietude in the middle of the morning's play.

This insistence upon our need for silence, quite apart from any definitely religious motive or object, seems elementary and pedestrian, but it needs reiterative emphasis in this age of loud disputes and weak convictions. The other day I chanced to talk to a strong, plain working woman whose mastery over adverse circumstances was little short of heroic. She had much to say concerning the simple habit of silence. "When I was a little girl," she remarked, "my mother taught me that a herbal tea was good for bruised flesh, and silence was good for a bruised soul; and she made me apply both whenever they were needed." Such homely wisdom, found more often in cottages than in mansions, has far more to do with the secret of our communion with God than we imagine. The soul that knows how to be silent in the ordinary fluctuations of life is the soul that will most readily master the art of spiritual quiet and recollection.

The church has still to learn what many a poor "crank" has learned long ago—that we frail, distracted children of humanity have no chance of hearing the voice of God until we have learned to be silent and listen. The spiritual realities do not shriek and shout, and it still remains true that Jesus comes with "the doors being shut." It was high wisdom, if poor exegesis, that made the mystical instinct interpret those shut doors as the resolute quieting of the soul that is necessary before the Christ can enter. When the saints and mystics desired the vision of visions, they first shut the soul's doors. It is not Christian liberty, but sheer dullness of spirit, that frees us from a wholesome fear of that "mixed multitude" of thoughts, concerns, and motives that turns the soul's sanctuary into a marketplace where the voice of Jesus is drowned out in the clamor of jangling impulses. Before we have any real right even to discuss the difficulties of communion with God, we must have resolved, at the cost of whatever hardship to our relaxed and dissipated souls, to learn the secret of silence.

III
THE POWER OF SILENCE

More especially we must learn to cultivate a deep reticence regarding the affairs of the soul. On this subject F. W. Faber's words are worth pondering:

> In spirituality, talking is always a loss of power. It is like steam. It is mighty when it is imprisoned, a mere vapor when it is set free. The "secret of the King" is dishonored when publicity is given to it, and it is no longer an element of earnestness, a source of fortitude within the soul. Hence it is that so few people have a sufficiently strong spiritual constitution to be able to indulge unharmed in conversation about their interior life and their mystical experience. . . .
>
> So also is it in good works. Many fine plans have been spoilt prematurely by making them public; not only because it was indiscreet, and has raised obstacles which would otherwise have been taken quietly and disarmed unawares, but also because we get tired of a thing which we talk much about. Our firmness goes off in talk. Our courage, too, is disheartened because of the chilling and adverse criticism to which we have exposed ourselves. Our power to persevere went with our divulging the secret.
>
> In like manner, charity is unqueened by all this

publicity. Everything that is lovely and heavenly about it is marred and disfigured, the bloom gone from it, the odor passed off, because its sanctuary has been invaded. . . . The tongue is a fountain that requires a huge water-power to feed it, and this power publicity seems abundantly to furnish; so that with that class of sins, a desperate, hungry, multitudinous, insatiate brood, the facilities are almost converted into necessities. But we not only want to give ourselves publicity, but to know the publicity of others. Hence our minds are filled with such a host of little details, scandals, gossips, rumors, hints, surmisings, interpretations, and judgments, that we are hardly able to practice the presence of God at all; and as to our prayers, distractions invade them with such irresistible regularity, that we can foresee and calculate the time when it will be no prayer at all, but all distraction.[3]

Who that has searched the deeps of his heart can doubt the truths of this? Our prayers are thin and perfunctory in exact proportion as our tongues are glib and gratuitously communicative. By the time we have talked a subject threadbare, we have evaporated its essence, and when at last we think of setting it before God, we are overtaken by a humiliating sense of emptiness and futility. The thing that had swelled to such gratifying dimensions under the genial influence of discussion is, in the light of the Eternal, seen to be a mere mote of small dust. As a matter of fact, we feel disinclined to pray about it at all, at least in private; and this is a healthy sign, for it means that there is at least one corner of our life in which we cannot tolerate a sham. It probably began as a reality, but we have talked it into a sham. It is no

---

[3] *The Blessed Sacrament*, pp. 250-51.

longer part of us. It is something quite external to our true selves—an occupation, not a vocation.

And if we trace this dismal business to its root, we shall find that what our habit of talking has done for us is really to undermine the very foundations of our spiritual life. If prayer has any reality at all, it is founded upon a sense of God, and as it develops into something more than an occasional spasmodic cry under the pressure of need or anguish, our sense of God becomes a dominant factor in our lives. We are learning the habit of referring everything to him, and measuring everything by his standard. But what does the love of talking do for this growing sense of God? Let Faber speak once more:

> What comes of this, but want of greatness? It is all so mean, so very little. For the love of publicity, interpreted spiritually, comes to this. The soul is so wearied of elevating itself to God, so tired of breathing the thin pure air of his presence, that it turns faint and leans upon the world, and makes the world its judge, its remunerator, its god; and the world lives on speed, feeds like a swallow as it flies, and cares for no harvest but swift results and the grandeurs of a night; everything becomes shallow about us, tall without girth, inconsistent, and insecure; everything must be run up, there is no time to grow. Novelties are wanted, and successes, and wonders, and sudden starts, and bold moves. All these things are the contradictories of the spiritual life.[4]

We are slow to realize that the so-called religious world is still—the world. Those who are inside that "religious" world are duped by it, and those who are outside are tragi-

---

[4] Ibid., p. 252.

cally prejudiced against religion itself by identifying it with that conventional religiosity the hollowness of which they are quick to discern. The Christian who lives in slavish deference to the religious world is, in effect, a living negation of the very soul of Christianity. It all runs back to this in the end: whether we mean to live in the light of God or in the light of the world. If we choose the latter, prayer becomes not only difficult, but, in its full sense, impossible.

What old spiritual writers used to call "human respect"— that enslavement to the opinion of our fellows which is responsible for nine-tenths of the futility of our lives—lies at the root, not only of our inability, but also of our more or less pronounced disinclination for solitary communion with God. Under its domination the world is always with us. We may enter into our closet and shut the door, that we may pray to our Father who sees in secret; but scarcely have we turned the key in the lock, when the omnipresent company invades our solitude, blotting out the divine Presence and filling the silence with a myriad of distracting tongues.

We are beset by an inquisitorial world-specter. It is as though the gaze of all humankind had been focused in one piercing, inescapable eye and concentrated upon our soul. To live beneath that intimidating glare is a slavery so galling that, as one has well said, the austerities of a Carthusian monastery might be easier to bear. It turns religion into an irksome imposition, if not into a positive torment, and makes of life a tawdry stage play—a hollow, heartless, spectacular affair, in which convention takes the place of right, prudential wisdom supplants character, and public opinion usurps the judgment seat of God.

This "human respect" is innate in every soul but gets its chance through the habit of ceaseless talk, and grows with the growth of our loquacity concerning things that are meant to be wrapped in silence. It is at once the most immature and the most noxious of our many present-day superstitions. "What have I gained," asked Emerson of his generation, "that I no longer immolate a bull to Jove, or a mouse to Hecate; that I no longer tremble before Eumenides, or the Catholic purgatory, or the Protestant judgment day—if I quake at opinion, the public opinion, as we call it, or at the threat of assault, or harsh words, or bad neighbors, or poverty, or mutilation, or at the rumor of revolution, or of murder? If I quake, what matters it what I quake at?"

In the end this love of talk, which at the worst we regard as an amiable weakness, breeds that cowardly and servile temper that is the exact opposite of dynamic prayer. For if prayer is indeed a great adventure, a giving of all for all, a staking of one's whole life upon an unseen good whose only pledge is the cross, then only the brave can pray. The essential servility of the talkative is, as a rule, concealed from us, because such persons have a very ambitious conception of what is due to them, and insist somewhat violently upon their rights. But, in reality, the soul that empties itself of its most intimate treasure in talk delivers itself over into a state of helplessness and slavery. Its clamorous self-assertiveness is the measure of its servile dependence upon the esteem and approval of its circle. Such a soul will never attain to vital communion with God. It may, indeed, have a remarkable facility in prayer—souls of this type are often temperamentally inclined to expansive devotions—but it will always stop short of the kind of prayer that transforms life into power and victory.

Abbot Alois, one of the Fathers of the Desert, maintained that "unless a man say in his heart, 'I and God are alone in the world,' he will not find peace"; and we need do no violence to our corporate consciousness and subscribe to a barren individualism in order to appreciate this saying. It expresses a profound truth of religious experience. Its logic is the logic of the heart. Everyone who knows anything about the interior life knows that there is indeed a moment in our communion with God in which the soul knows itself to be alone with him in the world, and knows also that in that august aloneness lies peace and power.

It was in his hours of solitary communion with the Father, when all other presences receded before the one over-shadowing, all-inclusive Presence, that Jesus heard the cry of the world's life and looked deep into its heart. It was then that he perceived the uttermost of human need and sorrow. "Close to the heart of the Eternal Father, he learned to love men, to see their misery, to understand God's purpose for them, to perceive the true meaning of sin. He leaves the world, and his reward is to know human life as none other ever knew it, to suffer, to pray, and to die for it."

"It is no small matter," says Thomas à Kempis, "to keep silence in an evil time." Sorrow may be among God's mightiest angels, but it does not necessarily, and in itself, do angels' work. A time of sorrow is often a time of moral and spiritual relaxation, of weakening self-pity, and of insistent demands upon the sympathy of others. The atmosphere of the house of affliction or mourning tends to become fixed on the illness. It breeds self-importance rather than heroism. And the selfishness of sorrow feeds upon speech. Small wonder that the masters of the spiritual life have always held up as the ideal what old writers used to call "the virginity of suffering"—the habit of keeping silence concerning our sorrows to all except God!

There is, of course, a limit to this counsel. Human sympathy of the right kind is sacramental, and God comforts his servants, as he comforted St. Paul, "by the coming of Titus."

But while past ages tended to deny the divine nature of human sympathy and fellowship, our own tends to idolize them. We again and again weaken ourselves and others, and miss the divine consolation, by running to this person and to that before we make our need known unto God. In the joy of our discovery of the sacredness of human affection, we forget that it remains unshakably true that whatever may be the power of human sympathy, the soul of humanity is created for direct, immediate communion with its God. Nothing, however lovely and true in its own order, can take the place of that immediate touch. And that touch will not be experienced by a soul that has exposed itself to every well-meaning hand, in its feverish search for comfort.

Did we but know the things that belong to our peace in times of sorrow and adversity, our instinct of spiritual self-preservation would urge us to hug silence to our bosoms and to reserve our deepest confidences for God. And of all sorrows, those of the inward life most urgently call for silence. The vice of airing one's soul to any and every person whom we believe likely to prove sympathetic and helpful is eating the very core of reality out of those who practice it. There are times in our spiritual life when we need a human counselor and guide, but nowhere are wisdom and self-restraint more imperative than here.

Our Protestant practice allows us to give free rein to our craving for sympathy, to pour out our confidences with as much profusion and intimacy of detail as we feel inclined to, and to go back upon the matter of our self-revelation as often as we choose, re-opening the same question again and again and keeping evil memories green. It is at this point that the Confessional makes its most valid claim, for one of its rubrics requires that the penitent pledge himself to refrain from ever discussing again what has once been confessed, either with his confessor or with anyone else. This is wise counsel, as anyone who has been concerned in the cure of souls well knows. And unless all who seek spiritual counsel, whether from a minister or from any trusty friend, are willing to abide by this rule, it would be far better to hide their spiritual wounds from every eye but God's.

IV
RECOGNIZING THE VOICE OF GOD

The most formidable enemy of the spiritual life, and the last to be conquered, is self-deception; and if there is a better cure for self-deception than silence, it has yet to be discovered. How many of the feverish motions, rooted half in the flesh and half in the nervous system, which we mistake for divine callings and inspirations would survive the test of silence? We have often been duped by some stirring of surface feeling, or temperamental passion which clothed itself in spiritual garb, when we might have known the truth had we taken our exaltation between our hands, as it were, and put it to the ordeal of silence. What pose, however unconscious, can co-exist with habitual silent waiting before God?

Nor is the result of this test merely negative. In nine cases out of ten, the unmasking of spurious vocations and impulses is all that is needed to let the voice of the true Shepherd be heard. That voice is always low and quiet. It often comes in and beneath the calls of ordinary duty. Yet it cannot be mistaken. Only a whisper, but the work is done; a foundation is laid upon which a new life can be built. Doubt as to the reality of our spiritual experience is our haunting besetment today, when popular psychology has invented a new species of mental torture by its talk of auto-suggestion and subjectivity and its mechanism of psychoanalysis. From that torture the sensitive among us will never escape, unless we resolve to be still and know.

And here it must be borne in mind that the silence we mean is not self-exploration and self-dissection, or that it corresponds to the process of psychoanalysis at the hands of an expert. Spiritual silence is the turning of the soul in quietness to a Power beyond itself. Self-analysis always breeds either a purely natural excitement—a mere effervescence of high spirits tinged by religious feeling—or else the dullness of self-despair. We are accustomed to defend a purely natural religiosity by way of reaction against the old-time orthodoxy which made human nature synonymous with evil. But while human nature is not evil, it is certainly, taken at its highest valuation, the good that is often the worst enemy of the best. Nothing can more effectually frustrate the transformation of human nature into that which God intends it to be than that same human nature content with its own goodness.

For generations we have made war upon a theology that denied the inherent goodness of human nature and made a virtue of self-disparagement. What is the result? Scarcely had we proved, with great satisfaction to ourselves, that the gloomy self-abasement and the groveling penitence of certain old-time saints were due to disordered livers, when laboratory psychology came along and bullied us into believing that spiritual elation was merely natural effervescence plus black coffee, or some less respectable stimulant. So we have come to question the reality of our spiritual exaltation, as we once questioned the reality of other people's spiritual depression. And it is only by the constant, patient effort to attain that stillness in which the voice of God can be heard that we shall ever find rest to our souls. If religion is of any value at all, it must be demonstrable beyond the reach of doubt—as demonstrable as that water wets or fire burns. And it is in the silence that our faith will be spiritually verified.

But how shall we recognize this voice of God, seeing that so many deluding voices call to us in the stillness? To begin with, we must be prepared to find ourselves making mistakes, and not to be discouraged by them. All life is a pursuit of truth against hazards, and the most false life of all is that which is forever seeking to guard itself against the risk of imposture. We are sent into the world by the God of brave men that we may, probably through many mistakes, learn to distinguish the voice of the true Shepherd from the voice of "strangers."

The alert and courageous soul making its first venture upon the spiritual life is like a radio operator on his trial trip in the Pacific. At the mercy of a myriad of electrical whispers, the novice at the receiver does not know what to think. How fascinating they are, these ghostly pipings and mutterings, delicate scratchings and thin murmurs—and how confusing! Now he catches the plaintive mutterings of an ocean liner trying to reach a French steamer, now the silvery tinkle from a Japanese gunboat seeking its shore station. There are aimless but curiously insistent noises, like grains of sand tumbling across tar paper: these are the so-called "static" noises of the atmosphere adjusting itself to a state of electrical balance. Again, comes a series of tuneless splashings—that is heat-lightning miles away—followed by the rumor of a thunderstorm in the opposite direction. Now he thinks he has got his message, but it is only the murmured greeting of ships that pass in the night. And then, just as his ear has begun to adjust to the weird babel of crossing sounds, there comes a remote and thrilling whisper that plucks at his taut nerves and makes him forget all his newly acquired knowledge. It is the singing of the spheres, the electrical turmoil of stars beyond the reach of the telescope, the birth-cry and death-wail of worlds. And when he is steeped soul-deep in the spell of this song of songs, there comes a squeaking, nervous spark, sharp as the squeal of a frightened rat. He decides to ignore it, and then suddenly realizes that it is calling the name of his own boat. It is the expected message, and he nearly missed it!

So the soul that waits in silence must learn to disentangle the voice of God from the net of other voices—the ghostly whisperings of the subconscious self, the luring voices of the world, the hindering voices of misguided friendship, the clamor of personal ambition and vanity, the murmur of self-will, the song of unbridled imagination, the thrilling note of religious romance. To learn to keep one's ear true in so subtle a labyrinth of spiritual sound is indeed at once a great adventure and a liberal education.

One hour of such listening may give us a deeper insight into the mysteries of human nature, and a surer instinct for divine values, than a year's hard study or external intercourse with people. That is why the great solitaries always surprise us by their acute understanding of life. Dwelling apart from people, they nonetheless have a grasp of human nature that the politician and the financier might envy. They are at home among its intricacies, have plumbed both its meanness and its grandeur, and know how to touch its hidden springs of action. And they know humankind because they know God and have heard his voice. To know God first and foremost is their distinction, and it can be ours, at the cost of simple, painstaking honesty with our Maker. Prayer of positive, creative quality needs a background of silence, and until we are prepared to practice this silence, we need not hope to know the power of prayer.

CHAPTER THREE

The Discipline of Meditation

A LITTLE WHILE AGO we were told that we had had enough of thinking about God; it was now high time to translate our thinking into practice, mobilize our forces, and "do something." Our young men and women had been captured by the ideal of service, and they were only waiting for a church that would give them something to do and lead them in the doing of it. It sounded plausible, and religious leaders dreamt of a large influx of candidates for the ministry and the Foreign Field, not to mention a host of young lay workers eager to strike out on lines of their own.

What actually happened, however, was the reverse of what these optimistic prophets predicted. Not only is there today[5] a tragic scarcity of volunteers for distinctly spiritual work, but even the most broadly humanitarian movements appeal for workers in vain. Child welfare, for instance, has become almost a shibboleth among progressive folk; yet one of the most advanced orphan institutions in England, where the best methods of child welfare are being tested on a large scale, finds

---

[5] The author is referring here to the conditions in England following World War I.—*Ed.*

it almost impossible to fill the vacancies on its staff. Social service, again, is the catchword of the altruistically minded; yet the head of a farm colony, conducted on the most modern and genially human lines, appeals in vain for young men to act as brothers to the colonists. Why this dearth?

The answer to that question cannot be given in any summary fashion; but there can be no doubt that one of the prime causes for this dearth of volunteers for service, in an age when the idea of service is held in almost superstitious reverence, is simply the lack of clear conceptions of the duty, the motive, and the end of true service. Professor D. S. Cairns has told us that in the Army there was scarcely one man in fifty who had any adequate knowledge of the fundamental principles and inward meaning of Christianity. There was a surprising amount of potential religion in the men, and a degree of essential goodness and pure unselfishness that was little short of amazing; but the impulse ran to waste, and the raw lump of religious feeling remained "unworked," and therefore largely unavailable, for sheer lack of elementary knowledge. In every department of life we give knowledge its due place. We do not, for instance, put a baseball bat in a boy's hand and toss him into the field without first teaching him the rules and showing him how to play. Yet we have sent a great army of men into life from our Sunday schools without having given them any more definite knowledge of religious truth than a vague feeling about God, half instinct, half superstition.

And when we turn from the man in the street to the man in the pew, we find very much the same state of affairs. True, he knows a great deal more about Christianity than his brother outside the church; but he knows it largely by rote, and as an abstraction separated from any close relation to the life he lives and the work he has to do. He knows after a fashion, but he has never been taught to think about what he knows, and to think about it in such a concrete, practical, acutely personal way as to make it truly his own. His prayer life is feeble and intermittent, and his response to the call for service negligible, for the simple reason that he really knows very little at firsthand about the God to whom he prays and whom he is called to serve.

Now this may seem as if we were playing with words. Experiential knowledge—the soul's firsthand experience of God—is something other than our intellectual apprehension of him, and to call both "knowledge" is to mislead. But while there is some truth in this, it must be borne in mind that the two kinds of knowledge are far from unrelated. Experiential knowledge of God may now and again come to a thoughtless, careless soul in a flash; but it will not grow, or become vitally influential, unless it is supported and built up by the steady application of the mind to the things by which men live. This does not mean an involved and ambitious intellectual process. The humblest peasant is capable of this steady application, and the restless philosopher, at home in the intricacies of a hundred rival systems, may fail in it completely.

To come to our own case. Behind all true Christian service—service, that is, springing from a sense of divine vocation and sustained by a supernatural motive—lies the interior life of prayer. And if that prayer life, and therefore the service that springs from it, is feeble and ineffective, it is largely because it lacks the background of genuine, honest thinking. "To think well," says Thomas Traherne, "is to serve God in the interior court." To pray well presupposes patient and systematic meditation, for meditation is nothing else than the art of thinking well and thoroughly upon the truths upon which prayer is based.

Such thinking has little in common with the mere desire

for information on religious subjects or with a talent for discussion; still less does it encourage a taste for controversy. It is the outcome of a settled resolution to come to grips with the great spiritual facts, by pondering them patiently and painstakingly steeping the mind in them, until the mind is as completely naturalized in their lofty atmosphere as it is in the air of the marketplace.

It may well humiliate us to reflect how nimbly, and with what instinctive precision, our minds move among the ordinary actualities of our life in the world, how sensitive they are to every change and how flexible in applying themselves to every new situation, and then to realize how awkward, blunt-edged, and unadaptable these same minds are when we try to apply them to spiritual reality. There is no avoiding the fact that it takes a strict and continuous discipline before the mind becomes tempered to the things of God, sensitive to the tides of grace, and flexible in the hands of the Spirit.

I

MEDITATION: WHAT IT IS

Like all great arts, the art of meditation is not easy, and those who expect their first fumbling attempts to yield a glow and rapture of soul are doomed to disappointment. The road is long and rough, and it is not the hearts of casual and impatient pilgrims that are made to burn as One talks with them by the way. The Christian soldier must make up his mind to endure hardness; it takes sweat of brain and soul before meditation can become a delight. In some cases, indeed, it never becomes delightful, and yet from that daily half-hour that seems so leaden and dreary, a hidden light will flow into the life.

Much has been written concerning the best methods of

meditation, and beginners are distracted by the multitude of counselors. A good method is a great help to most people, but in the end each one must discover his own method; and so long as that method includes an act of the will and the affections, and a definite practical resolution—one that can be carried out the same day, if possible—we need not worry unduly over matters of order and detail. The guiding thought that must govern our attempts is that meditation is not reasoning, or quiet musing, or preaching a sermon to ourselves, but a spiritual act as definite and purposeful as a business engagement, a pledge of friendship, or a solemn undertaking.

In our meditation we apply spiritual facts and principles to ourselves as individuals and as citizens of the Kingdom of God. We draw out how these facts and principles bear upon the particular concrete conditions of our own life and its problems. Having pondered them, we seek to appropriate their value by pouring out our loving desire toward God and by exercising our will in the forming of resolutions. A good meditation always results in a renewal of our vows from some fresh angle; we once again commit ourselves to God, and we pledge ourselves to his service under the impulse of the new thought or insight that has come to us, and in definite relation to the duty of the hour.

It follows that there is no room for ornamental fancy or eloquence in a genuine meditation. It may be profound and intellectually admirable, but even so it must remain quite simple and practical. Whether the person who meditates is a spiritual genius or a dull and poorly endowed soul, the one important question is whether the meditation will stand the wear and tear of common life. If it appears fanciful and visionary, once we have reached the office and plunged into the day's business, it was a failure, no matter how it made our hearts glow at the time. No meditation is really valid unless it leaves us with something to which we can return during the day's business and find it helpful there. This does not mean, of course, that we must deliberately aim at being dull and obvious in our meditation: what we must aim at is to be natural.

If the winged thought and the poetic imagery come naturally, and—what is of sole importance—if they express vital reality for us, they enhance the value of the meditation. But to seek them is to rob meditation of its true power. If we are indeed bent on facing reality, there is obviously no room for the deliberate cultivation of charm. The facts of the spiritual life are always beautiful, but their loveliness reveals itself only to the honest eye. They shine in their own light; to see them by the lantern of poetic fancy is to create a mirage.

Perhaps the most common difficulty about meditation is the choice of a topic. "With what shall I begin?" is the vexed question, especially for those who come to meditation somewhat late in life. There is only one safe answer. Begin just where you are; that is, with the subject that is of most interest to you at the present stage.

Do we come to meditation as lovers of nature, who have again and again seen God in some wayside flower? Then let us begin with that flower, seeking to yield ourselves up to the wonderful life behind it. Like Brother Lawrence, we may become new beings by touching nature's garment. "He told me," says his biographer, "that in the winter, seeing a tree stripped of its leaves, and considering that within a little time the leaves would be renewed and after that the flowers and fruit appear, he received a high view of the Providence and power of God which has never since been erased from his soul. This view had set him perfectly loose from the world, and kindled in him such a love for God that he could not tell whether it had increased in the more than forty years he had lived since." One might discourse very interestingly about the psychological condition which lay behind this remarkable conversion, but psychology helps us very little in undertaking such an adventure.

What we need is not to become versed in the psychology of the saints, but to get into touch with the objective reality that made them saints. There is a life, a revelation, in Nature, and if we humbly and quietly wait upon the power of that life and listen for the voice of the revelation, we shall not be sent empty away. We still like to speak of scientific law. There is no law so scientific as the law that if with all our hearts we truly seek God along the ways that are accessible to us, we shall ever surely find him. Communion with God is not an impressionist experience, an incalculable and fugitive emotion. It is based upon the uniformity of the divine nature, and if we insist upon approaching the quest psychologically, the only psychology we need to concern ourselves with is the psychology of man's response to an eternal and unchanging God.

Or if, perchance, we are lovers of little children and find a whole heaven in a baby's eyes, let us begin our course of meditation by setting a little child—maybe the child we love the best—in the midst of the contending multitude of our thoughts. We are slowly learning that "education" includes the education of parents by their children and of teachers by their pupils, and that the only way to approach a little child rightly is to open one's heart to its unconscious influence, to give oneself to the child in humble, unaffected trustfulness. And as we do this in the spirit of true devotion, we shall discern the mystery and wonder of the Child of Bethlehem. If we have ever really known and loved and studied one little child, we shall never again speak of God as the great "First

Cause" and "Architect of the Universe," and think of him as merely the personification of human progress and destiny. We shall know then that Christianity is the glad tidings of a Savior "wrapped in swaddling clothes, lying in a manger."

II

MEDITATION: FROM THE FAMILIAR TO THE UNKNOWN

But if it is well to begin our meditation with the sweet familiar things that have sunk most deeply into our lives, we must beware of ending there. We are all as sheep led by an unseen shepherd, and it is one of our most common fallacies to imagine that what attracts us most naturally and spontaneously is the thing that corresponds most closely to our deepest needs, and to reject as a survival of an irrational asceticism, any suggestion of bending our mind to the thing that does not attract. The new psychology, if nothing else, ought to convince us to the contrary. If the subconscious self means anything, it means that we are not necessarily aware of our deepest and most potent affinities, and that what we call our vocation may be only a superficial temperamental inclination and not the trend of our real nature.

The science of the saints anticipated modern psychology in this matter. Again and again the masters of the spiritual life tell us how a call, a vocation, came to them which seemed at first sight entirely uncongenial and often violently repugnant to their natural inclination and endowment. But as they followed it patiently and heroically, it became clear that the call that seemed so irrational was addressed to certain inner susceptibilities and sympathies, and to certain latent capacities and powers, which lay unrecognized in the depth of their being and would have remained unknown to them had not their brave obedience to the divine call brought them into conscious activity.

The same holds in the practice of meditation. Subjects that seem uncongenial are often found in the end to answer to an unknown need and to call forth an unexpected response. There is among us today a universal reluctance to meditate upon the great Christian doctrines—a reluctance that, as we have hinted already, is almost wholly because religious controversy has made us familiar with the objections to these doctrines before we have had time to understand the doctrines themselves. We approach them with a preconceived distaste. We are interested in the revolt of the modern mind against them, often forgetting that there has always been a "modern" mind, and it has always revolted. We seem to find it difficult to realize that the things against which that mind revolts are, to say the least, not uninteresting either.

Amid the babel of modern pronouncements on the Bible, we forget that the Book has a voice of its own—a message and a power that remain untouched by the passage of time. To listen to that voice and test that power for oneself is well worth all the labor and discipline involved, and to do so one must go to the "great texts." It may be pleasant and soothing to meditate upon the mountain symbolism of the Psalms, or on one of the many sweet humanities in which Scripture abounds; but such meditation will not go far towards enlarging and deepening our minds.

What we need is not to muse upon the psychological significance of David's playing on the harp when Saul was in an evil mood, but to ponder what Jesus meant when he said, "No one knows the Father but the Son, and those to whom the Son will reveal him." We need to wrestle with spiritual principles, to come to grips with the "hard sayings" of the Gospels and the tremendous paradoxes in the letters of St. Paul. Whether

our ultimate intellectual conclusions be orthodox or heterodox matters comparatively little; the one thing needful is to
clear our minds of the small dust of popular controversy and
approach the Book "with open face."

And this brings us to the subject of purely topical meditation. Nothing should keep us from applying our minds to
the great master-facts of the spiritual world—God, Christ,
the Holy Spirit, humanity, sin, graces, death, judgment, the
church holy and catholic, the Kingdom that shall have no
end. What do we really believe about these facts (what we
do not believe about them would probably fill a volume, but
is of little real concern, humbling though that fact may be to
us), and what is the effect of our belief upon our life? To
meditate upon the nature of God, for example, is not to con-
struct a theory of the divine nature, but to come into vital
touch with God himself through the intelligence.

In the course of such a meditation, we shall ask ourselves
some searching questions: "What do I really believe about
God when I am alone, in my private and secluded heart?
What do I believe about him in times of trouble and crisis?
What, in other words, is my working faith—the faith I
instinctively apply to the problems of life? How much of the
teaching to which I assent as a member of the church, or of
the sentiments I occasionally express in a study circle or
other meeting, has really entered into the fiber of my being?"

Such questions, if honestly faced, will take us out of the
region of merely individual conviction and experience; for
our answers to them will go to prove that while we are fully
cognizant of our own difficulties and problems and needs (at
least of the more superficial manifestations of them), we
really know very little about God at first hand. And at this
point our meditation ought to resolve itself into a state of
docile attention to the voice of God himself, a firm resolve

to know him better, and a sincere outgoing of our heart's desire to him. We then become aware that our conscious difficulties and needs are not the deepest and most real, and we shall feel impelled to turn from our known selves to him "to whom all hearts are open, all desires known, and from whom no secrets are hid"—the God who searches and interprets the subconscious self. We shall feel that there are in God whole worlds of grace and glory which have not entered into our personal experience, but which are nonetheless of supreme importance to us, both as individuals and as members of God's family. And if we are wise, we shall gird ourselves to explore these unknown tracts, for they will prove to be "our own country."

The task is not an easy one. At first we shall grope and stumble along a path lit but dimly and fitfully. Distractions—the chronic torment of those who wish to meditate—will drag us back at every step, and we shall often lose heart. But while we need to be severe with those recalcitrant minds of ours that are always going off at a tangent, we also need to remember that Christian meditation is not a drill in concentration or self-hypnotism. Distractions need not be hindrances. They may be, and often are, the raw material of a far more profitable meditation than the one they interrupt.

If, for example, during a meditation upon God, the thought of some harassing care or absorbing occupation recurs again and again, why not make that thought part of the meditation by seeking to learn how the spiritual fact we are pondering bears upon it? After all, the first requirement of a good meditation is not flawless logical sequence, but reality; many a supposed distraction is nothing else than the voice of God recalling us from mere speculation to reality. But while meditation must be related to personal problems, it must never be allowed to become either self-introspection or absorption in one's own problems. Self-love is the slum of the soul, and the supreme function of meditation is to lift us out of its squalor into the clear, pure air of the spiritual world.

III
MEDITATION: GROWING TOWARD SIMPLICITY

In meditation God grows upon us until we are saturated with the thought of him. At first the whole spiritual world seems a vague abstraction, but gradually, as we gaze with reverent, steadfast eyes into that infinite life from which we came and from whose exhaustless fountain the frail vessels of our lives are filled, we come to discern the beauty and splendor of that spiritual world. What was vague and empty is seen to be a full and wonderfully articulated reality. Gradually but surely, we become "familiar with the infinite riches of the many-sided idea which is God."

Perhaps it is the mystery of creation that first enthralls us. Of a sudden—we know not how, but we know it came by habit of fixed attention—we see creation as a romance, the wooing of the Eternal Lover. We discern the self-giving love in the heart of God when he made humankind. We see it take flesh in Jesus. How shall we name him who is the fountain of love, and him in whom the response of love became incarnate, and him who is the tide of love sweeping from God to humanity and from humanity back to God? What if, after all, the great catholic insight into the mystery of love that we call the doctrine of the Trinity holds that truth which alone can satisfy and build up our souls?

In something after this fashion, we may, through meditation, rediscover for ourselves the truths about God that some like to call dogma, but that are in reality seeds of life.

It will come to us that what theologians call the Incarnation means a revolutionary reorganization of humanity. Where before we relegated it to the region of dry doctrine, we find now that it is a principle the implications of which extend over the whole of the world's life. We realize that it pledges each of us to a way of life so new and wonderful that we shrink from its mingled glory and terror, while leaping to its thrilling challenge—a way of life so broad that it embraces the whole universe, and yet so narrow that there is no room in it for even a half-starved self. We also gain glimpses into the mystery of the Spirit's working. The Dove that hovered over the waters of Christ's baptism, the Pentecostal tongues of fire, the power that created the Body of Christ which is the church, become symbols of a living reality to be progressively appropriated in experience.

The Gospel story, which has become mere history—and legendary history at that for so many of us—now reveals its timeless value. Gazing upon Jesus in humble, loving meditation, we shall see the uncreated Life clothing itself with our human nature and taking the flickering torch of our mortality into its deathless glow. The nativity and childhood, the baptism, the temptation, the three years' ministry, and the passion and death of Jesus yield up their compelling significance to our waiting souls. We no longer see them, with dull eyes, as mere stages in the development of the greatest among the sons of men. Each shines for us with its own creative light, for from each there streams out a restoring and transforming energy such as can reside in no mere historical happening. Hampered no longer by the importunate irrelevancies of theoretical discussion, we adore the child Jesus with the shepherds of Bethlehem, and so learn the secret to which mere investigation, whether its results be orthodox or heterodox, has no key.

We know why the sages worshiped "when they saw the young child with Mary his mother." Each successive movement in the drama of our redemption appears in its own perfection and communicates its own gifts to our souls. Each makes its own demands and suggests its own method of approach. The contemplation of the Nativity initiates us into the path of humility. The stages of the three years' ministry impose their appropriate spiritual discipline upon us. The redeeming death reveals to us the pearl of penitence, and it exercises us in the theology of the broken and contrite heart. We shall not close our eyes to critical values; but we shall give critical inquiry its own place, which is a more important one than traditionalists dream of and a less important one than modernists like to think.

We shall find that as we go on, our meditations, instead of growing more elaborate and complex, will grow steadily simpler, one single thought often sufficing to fill the quiet half-hour. F. W. Faber has well said that one commonplace truth which would seem tame and trivial to the beginner suffices a saint for hours of contemplation. We have often marveled how simple, how almost childish, are the recorded devotions and aspirations of many of the mightiest spirits, and in what reverence they held certain books which we cast aside as too elementary and commonplace for our color-loving minds. But as we go on in the lowly way of meditation, we too shall become capable of that "loving, simple, sustained attention of the mind to divine things," which sees "a whole world in a grain of sand." That steadfast spiritual gaze and loving adherence of the soul to God, which caused St. Francis to find food for lifelong meditation in the one phrase, "My God and my All," is not a negation of the intellect, an artificial return to childish ways. It is rather an intellectual achievement (where intellect is not mere reasoning, but the exercise of the larger reason which includes spiritual imagination).

Such an achievement is akin to that of the scientist who can take in a large group of facts at one simple glance and almost instinctively synthesize them into a single unity. It belongs to the realm of that spiritual intelligence which is the very flower of thinking and reasoning. Nothing reveals the essential vulgarity of the restless impressionist mind more than the things that tire and bore it. In this sense, also, to love God with the brooding love that finds its absorbing occupation in the mere gazing upon the Beloved is a liberal education.

IV

MEDITATION: GROWING IN LOVE

We are thus led by the practice of meditation from the point where self occupies the center of our thought and we expect God "to revolve diligently round us," to the point where we become predominantly aware of God. We are now far more concerned about the claims of the love of God upon us than about even the most spiritual of our own moods and desires. God is becoming the central reality—the beginning, middle, and end of our prayer. All people have the power of seeing God and realizing his presence spasmodically in flashes, but the spiritual discipline of meditation raises what was an evanescent mood to a sustained habit.

If, then, we have been faithful in our meditation and not allowed it to become an occasion of self-seeking, we shall find that love of God—that steady and profound gravitation towards our Creator and Redeemer which is more than an emotion, and in which lies our very life—will be born in the heart. Who can compel love, we often ask, and how can we, whose spirits blow where they will, obey a command to love the Unseen? In meditation we may find an answer. We love God so little because we know him so imperfectly. Who loves a chance acquaintance? "We know and have believed," says St. John, "the love of God towards us." The unknown may, and does, exert an initial attraction, but our response depends upon our knowledge. In valid meditation that knowledge dawns and grows. Thoughts come to us that are no mere intellectual apprehensions, but that lay compelling hands upon emotion and will. Through them the love of God is shed abroad in our hearts, and before we know it we respond in some measure.

We *must* love, since he has first loved us. There is but one love, and it created as well as recreated us. To be made in God's image is to be made to love him, and to love him means life from the dead. The humblest act, then, becomes an offering of love—radiant, beautiful, exquisite as no work of art can be exquisite. Each word becomes mystical and holy because it is the impulse of love articulate. The meditation that does not waken love in our hearts, however poor and feeble that beginning of love may be, is imperfect; for where God and the soul really meet, there the intelligence, the will, and the emotions rise together, and what before was hearsay of conventional theology becomes self-evident truth. God reveals himself as the supremely loving and lovable One; and love, as Thomas Traherne reminds us, is continually communicating, propagating, and begetting itself.

We see now how far astray we are when we speak of the burning love of the saints for God as a medieval characteristic impossible to people of our day. The love of humankind for God is not the fashion of any age. It is grounded beyond the reach of change in the nature of God and humanity. Its expression varies from age to age, but its power persists unweakened; and the last lesson that the last person born on this earth must learn is that our sole dignity and happiness lies in learning to love our Maker and to serve him out of pure love.

The difference between the saints of old and ourselves is not one of inherent nature; it is simply that they took time to ponder God, to gaze upon him in an act of supreme attention in which intelligent will and desire concurred in perfect harmony, while we are too greatly overrun with small activities and occupations to find leisure for such pondering. Whether living in the earliest ages of desert spirituality or in the highest intellectual circles of our generation, every human being who has really set himself to live in the thought of God has felt the glow of a new affection, the unsealing of a fountain of love within.

And as we ponder and are silent, that Love will utter its unspoken demands. In some form or other, we shall hear the cry, "My child, give me thy heart." And on our answer to that cry hangs our destiny.

CHAPTER FOUR

From Self to God

IN DEFINING THE ESSENCE of prayer as the soul's loving intercourse with God, and its primary condition as detachment from self and attachment to the divine Friend, we seem to lay ourselves open to the objection that such intercourse issues in a dreamy mysticism. Life, they say, becomes a pious absorption in God, as selfish an affair as romantic absorption in a beloved human.

The validity of this objection depends entirely, however, upon the conception of God which is involved. If God is seen merely as the great Other, the soul's divine Counterpart; if, in short, our attachment to him is conceived of in terms of romance, then prayer must logically lead us into a cloistered and somewhat sickly pietism, separated from any relation to the world and its needs. But so to conceive of God is to converse with a phantom. God is not merely the mystic Lover: He is the Center of a whole world of eternal reality, and prayer involves the soul's discovery of that world and its progressive adjustment to its new environment.

This implies activity of the highest order—activity in which mind, will, and emotion work together at their highest potency.

If, further, we define God as creative and redeeming Love, his world of reality becomes the scene of his creative and redemptive activity; and prayer, far from alienating us from humanity, will give us a new understanding of it and a new concern for its destiny. It will commit us to take our share in the plan and purpose of a God who so loved the world that he gave himself for its redeeming. As we pray we shall, like George Fox, be "baptized into a sense of the conditions and needs of all men."

I

THE ONE THING NEEDFUL

But while creative prayer must result in a passion for humanity, it must begin with a single eye towards God. At the beginning of our prayer life we are self-centered. Prayer means little more to us than "asking." We ask for personal favors, for blessings upon ourselves and those belonging to us. In our prayer vocabulary personal pronouns occupy a disproportionate place. It is *my* needs, *my* relations, *my* friends; and even when we go further afield and pray for those whom we have never seen, it is because their needs have been so presented to us as to stir our sympathies and appeal to our idiosyncrasies. In the last resort, we still make use of God in prayer. What altruism we have is temperamental. It remains uninformed by a deep view of God and humanity, and it is limited by our natural affinities; our prayer, in fact, remains essentially self-centered. And it belongs to the pathos of our spiritual pilgrimage that so many sincere and noble souls never seem to get beyond the prayer of self-regard and self-reference.

Moreover, many of the new methods of prayer which profess to deliver us from the prison of self are seen, upon closer analysis, to be but subtle variations of the self-centered prayer. Not a few leaders of fashionable prayer cults make a point of insisting on complete concentration upon God as the prime condition of success. Human need, they urge, must be forgotten entirely. The devotee must, by intense mental abstraction and concentration, ascend to heavenly places, and think only of God in his inalienable omnipotence, indestructible peace, and inextinguishable joy. Only so shall his victorious and health-giving power be communicated to us, and through us to those for whom we pray.

But all the time the motive of this "giving out of oneself into God" is to gain relief from trouble, sickness, or sin. No less than frankly self-centered prayer, these cults make God not an end, but a means to an end. They name God, and intend self. They are on a level with the procedure of jaded society women, who seek to forget their fretting ambitions by steeping themselves in the regenerating simplicities of nature—not because they love nature, but in order to bring back luster to dull eyes and a healthy glow to faded complexions.

But in the normal course of our spiritual growth, there comes a time when the center of prayer shifts from self to God. Petition, in its narrower sense, recedes. True, it is not excluded, for nothing that touches us can be indifferent to our Father in heaven; and our Lord himself had a special love for plain, forthright, "unmystical" folk, who asked God for what they wanted as simply and frankly as they would ask their neighbor to help them out in a domestic emergency. But petition will no longer be the pivot upon which prayer turns. The true motivation will now be to get nearer God, to know him better, to experience his friendship, to enter more fully into his thoughts and purposes.

Self-centered prayer leaves us exposed to a thousand doubts and fears. Experience gives the lie to theory, and the sense of blessings withheld and requests ungranted lays a choking hand upon faith. We know not how to answer the sceptic who reminds us that his child, for whom he did not pray, recovered, while ours died. Books fail to reassure us, and we wonder if prayer is, after all, no more than a process of autosuggestion.

And all the time it is our fundamental attitude that is at fault. Prayer is simply intelligent, purposeful, devoted contact with God. Where that contact is established and sustained, prayer will "work" infallibly, according to its own inherent laws. But such contact cannot be established until we see God as the center of an eternal world of love in which we have citizen rights and duties, and until we act upon that vision. Failing this, the contact remains partial and spasmodic, and prayer, far from justifying itself, needs to be bolstered up by a hundred arguments, none of which succeeds in convincing even the apologist himself.

We need devise no elaborate theory or method of God-centered prayer. There is only one "rubric"—*the lifting up to God of our honest desire to know him and to be made one with him.* God-conscious prayer at its highest involves honest thinking, and a firm resolution to bring all our problems to the searchlight of his truth and to submit all our work to the touchstone of his interests and intentions. A lifelong discipline—intellectual, spiritual, and moral—is needed before we can call ourselves adept in creative prayer. Yet the least gifted and most poorly equipped soul can attain mastery in it; for, from first to last, simple, honest desire for the love and fellowship of God is the key to all its mysteries.

II

THE SHIFTING CENTER OF PRAYER

God-centered prayer, then, means to enter the world of reality. It may be defined as a progressive revaluation of the whole of life in accordance with a revolutionary experience which we have called the shifting of centers; but it is far better to approach it more simply, and conceive of it as a living way—the way of Love. For that world of reality of which God is the center is the world of enduring and victorious Love, and its highway—the great orienting path that gives it coherence—is Christ. "Your life is our way," says Thomas à Kempis; and the life of Christ in its eternal significance is indeed at once the way that each individual disciple has to tread, and the way of God in human history.

We are here in the region of that mystical "Christ-process"—the recapitulation of the birth, life, and death of Christ by the individual soul—which seems so remote and confusing to the plain person, largely because its exponents have clothed it in a difficult and esoteric jargon. But, in reality, it is quite simple—difficult, indeed, as all great things are difficult, but never remote from life or inaccessible to the average intelligence. It means that Christ did not come merely to be our example or our guide, but to live a new kind of human life, and to live it in such a way that each of us can live it after him in individual fashion. His life—the new order of living which he initiated—is a way, a path, the key to a new world. It can be understood only by living it after him; to view it externally is to miss it altogether.

> Though Christ a thousand times
> In Bethlehem be born,
> If he's not born *in thee*
> Thy soul is still forlorn.[6]

We know this is true. We may say that there is nothing mystical about it, that it simply means that we must have the

[6]From a poem in German by Angelus Silesius, 1624–1677.

spirit of Christ; but what could be more mystical than having this spirit of Christ—what more mystical, indeed, than the birth of love of whatever kind within the soul? How is this spirit possessed? The intellect cannot convey it to the life; mere willing cannot conjure it from the eternal deeps; burning emotion cannot fix it into our nature as an enduring principle. Proximity to Christ, alone, cannot give it to a person, or else Judas Iscariot would have possessed it, and every theologian would be a saint.

To say that the spirit of Christ comes by prayer, by the lifting up of a humble heart to God, is to say the most mystical thing of all. It is to affirm that prayer is supernatural. We shrink from using the term "supernatural," and we must concede at once that what we have called the supernatural life of prayer is truly natural, if nature be taken to include the divine-human as incarnate in Christ. But just as human thought and emotion are "supernatural" with reference to the animal world, so the life of creative prayer is supernatural in regard to the life we conventionally call human. Its impulse and sustaining power come from beyond ourselves. It is a divine mystery—the mystery of the birth and life, the dying and rising again, of Christ, recapitulated in the soul that prays. We need not describe this mystery in high-sounding terms; each event represents a stage in the process of the shifting of centers, the pilgrimage of the soul from itself to God.

Let us seek to trace this Way, which is Christ. Assuming that we have had some experience of self-centered prayer—genuine and fruitful as far as it went, yet essentially self-regarding—there comes a time when this way of prayer no longer suffices. The awakening may come through the intellect, or through the deeper emotions. It may be a sharp pain, or only a dull uneasiness. In any case, we feel the stirring of that buried life in the deeps below consciousness—the life that lies at once beyond and at the back of reason and will, unrecognized by us, yet capable of using our faculties. The discovery of this hidden element in our being may at first lead to nothing more than a revolt against institutional religion. We feel unsatisfied with what churches and religious systems have to offer. They do not meet our new needs; the remedies they possess do not touch the aching nerve of our being.

At this stage we shall be tempted to turn from organized forms of spirituality and to seek refuge from the repugnances of the corporate Body of Christ in the solitude of our own spirits. In this there is danger, however. It is but a plausible version of the satanic temptation, "If you are the Son of God, cast yourself down, for he shall give his angels charge concerning you." Our safety lies, not in separation, but in loyalty. It is precisely when the church appears to have the least to offer us, that our wisdom lies most surely in remaining within her courts; for we may be certain that the soul that finds nothing but emptiness within the collective experience and life of believers will find nothing but hallucination and delusion within its solitary self.

In such hours we need the utmost self-restraint and the most humble attention to the voice of God. We do not know what is being wrought in us; we cannot see the holy thing that surely will be brought to birth, if only we say from our hearts, "May it be to me as you have said." We are conscious only of restlessness, dissatisfaction, peevishness. The house of selfhood is being demolished over our heads. What satisfied us before inspires us now with weariness and distaste. The shell of natural religiousness has cracked, and our unloveliness obtrudes. We are drawn to pray in the Spirit, but realize that there can be no "my" or "mine" in such prayer, whereas we are full of "my" and "mine."

This is a period of painful incubation, and it may be

spoiled by a single touch of self-will. Nothing avails here but perfect docility. A demand is being made upon us—the demand for obedience, and for that royal generosity which gives all for all, asking nothing back. Our response to that demand will depend upon our willingness to cease from self, and upon our loyalty to that deeper life the stirrings of which we can only half understand.

III
A NEW VIEW OF THE WORLD

Then, perhaps by a sudden, sharp invasion of a new life flooding ours from without, as it were, or by the sudden rising of the flood from within the deeps of the spirit—probably by the meeting of both—we become conscious of the birth of the Christ-spirit within ourselves, and of our own birth into a new and wonderful world. Or the process may be of the most gentle and almost imperceptible nature. A brooding stillness about us, the coming of light we know not how, the sacramental renewal of soul by an element that drops upon it as silently as manna—in these, and in countless other ways, some of them inexpressible in words, the new life comes. But however it comes, it means the soul's emergence into a world familiar, yet almost frighteningly unfamiliar—a world in which we feel utterly strange and awkward, and which we yet recognize as our true home.

It is the world of which God is the center. We look upon him, and our life is renewed. We are given a set of new values, a spiritual coinage other than that with which we have hitherto traded. Things that but a little while ago seemed desirable now appear as dross. Things we recently dubbed peculiar and fanciful suddenly become entirely natural and solidly substantial. We discover untold beauties in God; we find in Christ secrets of final restitution that fill us with death-less hope. Matter is seen to be the storehouse of unguessed spiritual treasure, a hiding place of holy powers, a laboratory of divine alchemy. Everywhere we see mysteries of healing and regeneration, of individual transfiguration and of world renewal that remained hidden while self was our center.

And as these revelations unfold themselves, the world we once lived in appears as a shriveled shell, a mere travesty of reality mocking us with its pathetic makeshifts for power and joy. We have become dead to a whole universe of delights and sorrows, and alive to an entirely different range of thoughts and emotions. It is as though we had developed a new set of faculties of appreciation and distaste, pleasure and pain.

While our birth into the new world is full of Bethlehem joys, it also, like Bethlehem, involves a sword that shall pierce us through. Our friends and neighbors cannot understand the thing that has come to pass in us. They call us odd, unreasonable, altogether irritating, if not enraging. Scarcely has the angel's song died away, when we hear behind us the footfall of our kinsfolk who call us mad, and of our enemies who say, "He has a devil." This spells pain, but it is a wholesome pain. It wakes us out of our selfish preoccupation with our experience and forces us to take our brethren into our thought. Above all, it puts the reality of our experience to the test. Every genuine experience of new life in Christ has this in common with the sterile extravagances of religious self-delusion: that both excite the ridicule and opposition of the worldly and of the merely conventionally religious. Both beget a sense of lone-liness and plunge the soul, fresh from the glow and rhythm of its rapture, into the chilling waters of petty criticism.

It is the manner in which we meet this check to our new-found joy that proves the validity or otherwise of our experience. The soul that has passed through a merely aesthetic and emotional process either will be betrayed into hostility against its critics, or it may take refuge in the calm contempt of the artist for the Philistine, wrapping itself in its own sensations and ignoring the jibes of the vulgar herd.

But he in whom the Christ has been born knows neither resentment nor contempt. Far from allowing his spiritual experience to alienate him from his brethren, he sees in their misunderstanding of him an added claim upon his sympathy. For as Christ was born into the world, not to stand apart from the common life of humanity as a judge, but to share it as a brother, subjecting himself joyfully to all the limitations and pains such a fellowship involved, so he in whom Christ's spirit dwells will steadfastly refuse any form of religious or mystical exaltation that releases him from the hampering influence of common relationships. The dull-souled who sneer and jibe at him, and the ill-willed who meet him with anger and malice, will have no judge more lenient, no interpreter more sympathetic, than the subject of their ridicule or enmity.

At the very threshold of a sharply individual experience, the soul that is truly submitted to God will realize its oneness with all persons. It is not a question of cultivating the corporate feeling, as if it were something added to a person's experience of Christ. God sees us not merely as individuals, but also in an ideal relation to our fellows; as the love of God is shed abroad in our hearts, we shall freely and generously identify ourselves with the weakest and most wayward, bearing their burdens and taking them into the very center of our prayers. The self-deluded soul goes forth in search of a spiritual romance, an emotional adventure that exalts it above other souls; but the soul in whose depths Christ is truly born covets not spiritual privileges that make for isolation, but rather refuses to be made perfect without its fellows.

Here is the final test of religious experience. No matter

how glorious the soul's adventure may be, whether in the realm of mystic feeling or intellectual apprehension, if it does not mean a passing out of self into that life of God which is world-embracing love, it is nothing, and worse than nothing. When we adopt the language of the mystics and represent the soul's pilgrimage as a "recapitulation" of the life of its Lord, we do so because that life was fundamentally a surrender of self, and each event in it was a stage in the process of deepening surrender.

Mystics have erred in treating the Christ-process as if it exhausted all spiritual experience, instead of representing it as only one of several ways of symbolizing that experience. They also have erred in applying the events of our Lord's life in rigid sequence and pedantic detail to the life of the soul. Needless to say, such a procedure is artificial and is calculated to prejudice sensible people.

There are as many ways of recapitulating Christ as there are souls. To some the Transfiguration, for instance, will become a center of experience, leaving its mark upon the whole life. Others will, at some great crisis of their lives, be remade by the reality embodied in our Lord's temptation in the wilderness. One will appropriate the mystery of Cana, and find the secret that turns all life's water to wine; another will be initiated into the sacrament of the baptism in the Jordan. Some find nearly every event of Christ's life reflected in their experience, while many more can trace no such detailed correspondence, and yet are able to say with St. Paul that they were crucified with Christ and are risen again with him.

The one universal element which pervades all experience is the emergence of a new life, with standards and values of its own, involving a progressive discipline, in which the self-principle is slowly put to death, and God becomes the center of the whole life.

IV
A DANGEROUS DELUSION

As we become naturalized in the world of divine reality, we shall be surprised to find that, instead of an ever-increasing fervor and delight in communion with God, our prayer life will sooner or later be characterized by "dryness" and depression. We shall cease to feel the presence of God. Our quiet hours will become disconcertingly bleak and barren of tangible result. Our meditations will be unfruitful, blighted by distraction and poverty of thought. Prayer will die on our lips, and we shall lose all sense of contact with God. If we have been accustomed to regard a sense of joy and exaltation, and an abiding consciousness of communion with God, as the tests of a genuine prayer life, we shall feel that we have been deceived in ourselves and will be tempted to give up the quest.

A great deal of religious literature is based upon the assumption that the way of true prayer is a way of ever-increasing spiritual delights, and much religious biography leaves us under the impression that the reality and depth of sainthood are to be judged by the degree of fervor in devotion and of joyous assurance which characterizes the life. It is the old vice of religious romanticism, which measures the spiritual life according to its richness in storms of religious emotion and tides of mystic passion. Such a criterion might be valid, if the object of the spiritual life were self-expression—the development of the religious temperament, the assertion of the spiritual ego. But if the object is the soul's pilgrimage from self to God, such a test is seen to be entirely beside the mark.

Three-fourths of our difficulties about prayer in its most spiritual aspect would disappear if we realized the simple truth that prayer is a dying to self and becoming alive unto God, and that each stage of a progressive prayer life is a stage in the putting to death of self, so that God may work and reign. The stages may be many and subtle, or few and clearly observable by all; in any case, they will be recognizable as so many aspects of God's holy war against self-love.

At the beginning, when prayer is still in its self-centered stage, we cling to material pursuits and pleasures. Then comes the birth of Christ in us, and we are weaned from these delights by the inrush of spiritual joys. A new range of pleasures has become ours, and our former delights appear dull and worthless. And in our absorption in the delights of the spirit, we imagine that we have left self behind for ever. It is all so new, so entrancing—we cannot get enough of it! Trouble and adversity fail to quench our infant joy; "what matters treasure, what matters pleasure," so long as we have the riches of God for our own?

But self is not dead: it has merely lost consciousness of its existence for a season, in its absorption in a new object of desire. It clings to its spiritual treasure as it once clung to the goods of earth. It is only when God withdraws these spiritual possessions from us that we realize how large a part self played in our holding of them. One by one they leave us—the first joy and fervor, the first well-nigh intoxicating sense of God's presence, the first inrush of unconquerable might and dauntless confidence.

They are taken from us, not harshly, but to make room for something less vivid and joyous, yet even more solidly sustaining—a deep, calm peace, a sense of perfect rest in God. We know why the first gifts have been withdrawn: it was that we might gain that self-knowledge which is power. We had grasped them too feverishly; their continuance could not be wholesome in the long run. They were the blossoms of springtime, and it is fitting that the riot of spring, the song of the rising sap, should give place to the calm, sunlit stillness of summer. We find, as we go on, that this new stillness of peace has a charm all its own. It, no less than the exuberance of joy, is a luxury. How gladly we let ourselves sink into its depths! It is worth feeling a little sober and pensive to experience such peace, since it makes us aware of the Everlasting Arms. A sense of satisfaction grows upon us, a fullness as of deep, still water filling a pool. We think that we have stripped ourselves of ambition: in quietness and confidence we have discovered our strength.

But again it is self-love that hugs this white peace of God to its arms, for we never really become aware of the depth of our self-love until God begins to tear it out of our hearts. Now peace, in its turn, is taken away from us, and we go forth into an arid wilderness. Our spiritual imagination fails, our feeling is numbed, words forsake us, thought is clogged, our spirits faint within us, and the heart is left as cold as last year's nests. We know not what to do. We have lost, not only self-confidence, but self-resource. God has withdrawn his hand, and we are left desolate.

It is at this stage that the temptation to turn back and renounce the pilgrim's habit becomes a real danger. At other stages this temptation arises from fickleness; it is but one mood among many. Now it springs from a vision of grim reality. For the first time we see ourselves as we are apart from God—naked, impotent, dead. At last we know that we can find no rest in self, and God—how far away God has withdrawn himself!

But this hour that seems so evil is the hour of our salvation. In it, as in nothing that has gone before, God is surrounding us with the purifying and healing energies of love. The shadow that frowns above us is the shadow of his hand; the emptiness that yawns within is his sure prophecy of a wondrous fullness. If we are being straitened, it is that we might be the more greatly enlarged. In withdrawing his felt presence from us and making us to know that without himself we can do nothing, God desires to dilate our hearts by loving and longing and so enable them to receive the fuller self-revelation which he longs to impart. If we are willing to walk through the wilderness of spiritual aridity, if without impatience or bitterness we turn our dull and empty hearts to God in a simple movement of love, we shall discover the wonders that are wrought in that desert of the soul.

Our greed for that sensible warmth of religious feeling, miscalled "experience" in some quarters, is one of our most dangerous enemies. We constantly hark back to the radiant happiness of the early Christians, point to the palpable gladness that throbs through the apostolic narrative, and say that spiritual life must be like that; if we lack joy, we lack God. But we forget that joy does not come by seeking it. "Seek God, not joy," is the motto of the saints, and it is the experience of the saints that those who truly seek God shall be led to joy in God's own time.

To the early Christians, who embraced God with perfect simplicity, asking no questions, giving not a look behind them, and selling the whole field of the world for the pearl of great price, joy came immediately; for joy is the reward of complete surrender, and God never keeps one waiting unduly. But we, hesitant, sophisticated, torn between rival theories and allegiances, making a study of self-analysis and self-expression, do not, as a rule, make this complete surrender until, by pain and desolation, the heart has been purged of its idols and the roots of self-love cut out of the soul. It is then, and only then, that joy can come. The way to it may be long and hard, but the moment the last step is taken and the life wholly yielded up to God, joy such as we have never known—radiant, triumphant, immutable—becomes ours.

V
AN ARID TWILIGHT LAND

It is not easy for us to accept the idea of an arid twilight land, for we are slow to relinquish the notion that prayer is a form of spiritual enjoyment, or at least a source of spiritual satisfaction. We do not realize that while a vivid consciousness of God, a flood of spiritual joy, the touch of inspiration and the flame of fervor are all valid and desirable elements of prayer, they are not of its essence—they certainly are not its central object. Some of the most profound spiritual writers go so far as to confine such experiences to the immature stages of prayer. They are the marks of the neophyte in Christ—the sugarplums awaiting spiritual babes to tempt them to take the first step. While we need not concur in a judgment that is not borne out by Christian experience, we shall do well to recognize that vivid emotion in prayer is one of the most fruitful sources of self-deception, and therefore one of the most formidable hindrances to true progress.

Prayer, we must remember, is, first and foremost, an act of devotion; and devotion is not an affair of fervid feeling or tender sentiment, but a solemn act, whereby a person devotes, commits, and consecrates himself wholly to God. Now, if such consecration means anything, it means the death of that self-will and self-love which separate the soul from its true Source; and that type of prayer is surely best which most effectually mortifies our lower self. No one who has had any experience of the spiritual life would maintain that prayer which is accompanied by a feeling of intense satisfaction and emotion is the most likely to purge us of self-love.

On the contrary, the danger of such prayer is that it gives self-love a unique opportunity. Self feeds on emotional prayer, and gradually we forget that we are on pilgrimage from self to God. We make no spiritual progress unless prayer becomes increasingly a fight to the death between the self that battens upon emotional luxury, and the love that claims that self as a living sacrifice. The central thing in prayer is not the garden of the soul, but the altar of dedication. If we can go to that altar with joy and singing, happy are we; but more blessed are those who ascend its steps in the nakedness of faith, giving all for all and asking nothing in return, save that the will of God may be fulfilled in them.

It is well therefore that after we have made the great dedication, we should be led into that arid twilight land where our schemes miscarry and our judgments mislead us, where emotion withers and will is seen to be but a broken reed, where we grope and totter and fall until we realize how frail was the staff of self upon which we had leaned. Mistrusting ourselves, we learn to put all our confidence in God. For the end he has in view for us is not to restrict us, but to set us free. We are stripped of self-resource, not that we might be humiliated, but that we might discover the unguessed resources we have in God. It is not the reflex influence of "dry" prayer in making us wiser and sadder that is its central significance, but such prayer's revelation of God as the one true life. If true prayer, so far from being a luxury, is one long crucifixion (as de Caussade has it), it is with Christ that we are crucified, so that we might live with him and he in us. We give thanks for "dry" prayer, not because there is any virtue in "dryness" or dullness, but because in it we are stripped of delusion in order that we might possess the supreme Reality.

Thou art oft most present, Lord,
      In weak, distracted prayer;
A sinner out of heart with self
      Most often finds thee there.
For prayer that humbles sets the soul
      From all delusions free,
And teaches it how utterly
      Dear Lord, it hangs on thee.
Thrice blessed be the darkness, then
      This deep in which I lie;
And blessed be all things that teach
      God's dear supremacy.

So far, then, from being a crushing and narrowing experience, this "dryness" in prayer, with its revelation of the supremacy of God, is a great emancipation. We emerge from it as slaves set free by God. We are no longer the slaves of our devotional moods, our religious prejudices and predilections. We have escaped the domination of all those superstitions which our regard for reputation and influence, our desire to appear consistent, and our love of another's praise have so long imposed upon us. Ambition no longer tempts us; human judgment ceases to intimidate us. We are delivered from the disabling fear of failure. Raised above the attractions and inhibitions of conventional religion, we partake, in some measure, of the glorious immutability of God himself. Our wills are tempered to steel. It was said of the early Jesuits that "when once the saints of the Society said, *I will*, the thing was done"; and this has always been true of those whose strength is rooted in the cross, where self has been crucified with Christ.

If a will of iron represents one aspect of the liberated soul, flexibility and detachment of spirit represent a complementary aspect. To obey the inspirations of grace moment by moment, adjusting oneself readily to the promptings of a living Master, is a task that demands the glorious liberty that is the high prerogative of the children of God. Complete docility to the divine Guide, instant response to his most fragmentary suggestions, and unhesitating readiness to go where he sends us, even though the call of today seems to contradict the command of yesterday—such flexibility requires a royal heart of devotion which defies human canons of consistency and looks to God only. Such a heart is not born in a person until he has been in that dark and secret place where he dies to self that he may live to God.

St. Philip Neri will always remain the classic example of this superb courage of obedience. He had no set rules or methods, no religious peculiarity of his own. He joined no monastic order, and would have no vows in the congregation that he founded. He had no "views," made few plans, and was ready to give up what he was doing at any moment. He took no thought for his spiritual career, but simply exposed himself to God's action upon him day after day, not in an attitude of sterile quietism, but in the spirit of joyous cooperation.

And it is little to be wondered that this quiet, jocund, free-and-easy man, who was so unconcerned about "giving edification," and so utterly detached from everything that was a means and not an end, exercised an almost irresistible attraction over his contemporaries, winning them from sin and worldliness, subduing their lusts, calming their fears, molding them to Christian ways, entering into their lives with the transforming ministries of the gospel as noiselessly and naturally as the sunlight enters a window at dawn.

The person who is freed from self and has found his true life in God is free indeed. He is untroubled by anxiety even about the affairs of the Kingdom of God. He is never hurried, does not seek place and power, is patient with himself as with others, and takes his faults and failures quietly. There is nothing showy or theatrical about such a person. His life is hid with Christ in God, and hidden from no one more than from himself. Coventry Patmore has given us an inimitable portrait of such a person:

> The saint has no "fads," and you may live in the same house with him and never find out that he is not a sinner like yourself, unless you rely on negative proofs, or obtrude lax ideas upon him and so provoke him to silence. He may impress you, indeed, by his harmlessness and imperturbable good temper, and probably by some lack of appreciation of modern humor, and ignorance of some things which men are expected to know, and by never seeming to have much use for his time when it can be of any service to you; but, on the whole, he will give you an agreeable impression of general inferiority to yourself. You must not, however, presume upon this inferiority so far as to offer him any affront, for he will be sure to answer you with some quiet and unexpected remark, showing a presence of mind—arising, I suppose, from the presence of God—which will make you feel that you have struck rock and only shaken your own shoulder. If you compel him to speak about religion, . . . he will most likely dwell with reiteration on commonplaces with which you were perfectly well acquainted before you were twelve years old; but you must make allowance for him, and remember that the knowledge which is to you a surface with no depth is to him a solid. . . . I have

known two or three such persons, and I declare that, but for the peculiar line of psychological research to which I am addicted, and hints from others in some degree akin to these men, I should never have guessed that they were any wiser or better than myself, or any other ordinary man of the world with a prudent regard for the common proprieties. I once asked a person, more learned than I am in such matters, to tell me what was the real difference. The reply was that the saint does everything that any other decent person does, only somewhat better and with a totally different motive.[7]

The spirit of hiddenness and the grace of doing common things in a supernatural way—these are the marks of the person who has been created anew. Prayer that does not stamp these marks upon the soul is greatly to be suspected.

VI

SELF-SURRENDER OR SELF-LOVE

Here we come to the heart of our subject. To have passed from self to God means to possess the spirit that does everything for the pure love of God—the spirit that made God as real to Brother Lawrence among his pots and pans in the kitchen as on his knees before the Blessed Sacrament. It transmutes every action into an offering of love, makes of every homely gesture an act of pure worship. In reading such a record as that of Brother Lawrence, we are struck by the simplicity of his religion. He has no theology, no elaborate ethic, no method of self-discipline; his only doctrine is the doctrine of doing one's daily work, even to the picking up of

[7] *The Rod, the Root, and the Flower*, pp. 160-62.

a straw from the floor, with a motive of love to God and as an act of devotion. It appeals to our preference for an undogmatic Christianity, and to our sense of the sacredness of what we call secular. It is such a practical faith, we say, so well within the reach of everybody.

But when we come to practice such a faith, we find that its simplicity existed only in our imagination. It is quite easy to believe that there is no limit to the creative power of one homely act of service done for the love of God, that it contains sufficient dynamic to break the whole life in pieces and make it anew after a divine pattern. We believe it because we have seen reflections of this glory in the most unlikely places. We have seen a poor seamstress, for instance, stitching away at her ill-paid labor in sullen resentment and dull defiance, and then seen her stitching away even more busily for her little child, and we have bowed before the omnipotence of transmuting love which can change leaden toil to golden delight at one touch.

However, when we come to practice the presence of God after the manner of Brother Lawrence, we find it an impossible business. Surely there is a flaw somewhere. Whatever may have been true of Brother Lawrence's time, we cannot solve the problem of life today after this fashion, by acquiescing in degrading work or unjust conditions of labor for the love of God. If we are fellow-workers with God, we demand in his name the right to tasks worthy of his partners.

There are two reasons for the difficulty we experience in translating the golden precept of Brother Lawrence into terms of present-day life. To begin with, we are so deeply imbued with the modern ideas of self-expression that we will not acquiesce in uncongenial work and hampering conditions. And while our discontent may not be wrong, its motive certainly is. If we are to rebel against our work, it must be, not because that work does not express ourselves, but because it does not express what we believe to be God's thought and will for us. We must choose between the ideal of self-expression and the ideal of vocation—the call to express God. The collision between the two ideals is sharp and radical, and it seems at first sight as if to surrender our right to self-expression would be to stultify the humanity which God has given us. But a deeper view resolves the contradiction. Who, for instance, is the true artist—he who goes to Nature to use her as a means of self-expression, or he who approaches her as a humble servant, seeking to record a fragment of her creative profusion simply because the truth of her is so beautiful? Who is the great writer—he who looks to his writing as a means of making him famous, or he who loses all personal ambition in his desire to interpret life simply because of his reverence and love for it? The answer is obvious. And the same holds true in the spiritual life. The true master is he who is so bent upon his art—the loving realization of God in terms of life—that he forgets the medium.

But a deeper reason for our difficulty is found in the fact that there is no merit whatsoever in choosing uncongenial work, or in persevering in it, unless that work really be our vocation. Most of those who quote Brother Lawrence miss this point. They seem to think that what he intended to teach was that any and every kind of work we happened to be engaged in was to be continued with a new motive; that the secret of possessing God was simply to go on with one's old work, but to do it henceforth from a motive of pure love. But, as a matter of fact, Brother Lawrence's own work in the convent kitchen was not his old work. He had been for many years a servant to a nobleman, and it was under a sense of divine vocation that he entered a monastery as a lay brother and was set to work in the kitchen. Nothing in his life or teaching supports the notion that sanctity consists in trying to "supernaturalize" work that is not our true vocation and that we can leave if we choose. Its only legitimate application is either to work that is our vocation, or to work that we cannot escape.

However, we have all but lost the sense of vocation. We often find ourselves in uncongenial employment, simply because we chose it in self-will at a time when it appeared congenial, and we were persuaded that we would always find it so. Or else we remain in uncongenial employment into which we were thrust by circumstances, not because these circumstances continue to be insuperable, but because a change would mean financial loss and sheer hard toil for years to come.

Here is a youth, for instance, who was conscious of a call to be a doctor, but owing to inescapable circumstances, had to break off his studies and become a clerk. Today these circumstances are less unmanageable. He could, by dint of hard work and the most frugal of living, attain his first desire. However, the prospect of giving up a steadily rising salary, or of sacrificing his comparatively ample leisure, or of being criticized and set down as "cranky" for starting at the bottom of the ladder when he was half-way up already, deters him from following his vocation.

It is not too much to say that two-thirds of those who plead uncongenial work as an excuse for their lack of spiritual joy and vigor could change their employment tomorrow if they were willing to pay the price. Certain it is that Brother Lawrence did not have them in view when he declared that there was no work so mean and humdrum but that a person could realize the presence of God in it. Still less sympathy would he have shown to those who imagine that they can practice the presence of God while engaging in dishonest or questionable occupations, or indeed, in any occupation, however harmless in itself, about which their consciences are in doubt.

The whole question of vocation is intimately connected with prayer; and many an aspiring soul finds prayer a weariness, if not a torture, simply because he lacks the courage to face the question as to whether his daily work is in a line with his true vocation. "The trivial round, the common task," will not in itself "furnish all we ought to ask." If mending shoes runs counter to God's will for us, it will prove as inimical to our spiritual life as the most ambitious self-chosen career. Self-will, or sheer spineless drifting with the tide, is every bit as wrong in the cottage as it is in the palace, and to remain in the kitchen from sheer laziness and cowardice is as reprehensible as to usurp the throne out of motives of greed and ambition.

It all runs back to the question that lies at the root of the spiritual life: Is the central element in our communion with God an act of self-surrender, or is it, on the contrary, a demand of self-love? Is the symbol of our prayer the open hand, or the open heart? Are we using God as a means of self-realization, or are we offering ourselves as a means of glorifying him? And if we mean self-surrender, has our offering been made in an honest, generous spirit, unconditionally and without reservations? Have we interpreted it emotionally, or are we seeking to work it out in the affairs of daily life?

Upon our answer to these questions will depend whether our spiritual life is a sectional, sophisticated business, an eccentric new patch on an old garment, or the transmuting of the whole life into the life of God. Our prayer life will be creative just as far as our whole life is charged with the creative energy of God. We need not waste our time in asking for the apostolic power in prayer until we have learned to say with the Apostle, "I live; yet not I, but Christ lives in me." From beginning to end, it is the presuppositions behind prayer that we need to be chiefly concerned about. Let the *law* of prayer be observed, and its *method* can take care of itself.

Our preoccupation with theories and ways of prayer is as superficial and essentially unintelligent as the superstitious insistence of certain revivalists upon "knee-drill." There is only one thing indispensable—a soul willing to let go of self and to live henceforth in God. "The mark of a saint," Bishop Westcott reminds us, "is not perfection, but consecration. A saint is not a man without faults, but a man who has given himself without reserve to God." And, rightly understood, one act of self-surrender can make a saint. Here is our only true wisdom in prayer, and here the only method that is of universal application.

Ah! if you adored a God crowned with roses and with pearls, it were a matter nothing strange; but to prostrate yourselves daily before a crucifix charged with nails and thorns—you living in such excess and superfluity of the flesh, dissolved in softness—how can that be but cruel? . . . He is cold and naked; he is alone; behind him the sky is dreary and streaked with darkening clouds, for the night cometh—the night of God. . . . He is crowned with thorns, but you with garlands; he wears nothing in his hands but piercing nails; you have rubies and diamonds in yours. Ah! Will you tell me you can still be faithful though in brave array? . . . Love which cannot suffer is unworthy of the name of love.

J. H. Shorthouse

"Lord, how often shall I resign myself? and
wherein shall I forsake myself?"

"Always, and at every hour; as well in small
things as in great. I expect nothing, but in all things
I will thee to be found naked. Otherwise, how canst
thou be mine, and I thine, unless thou be stripped of
all self-will both within and without. . . .

"I have very often said unto thee, and now again
I say the same: Forsake thyself, resign thyself, and
thou shalt enjoy great inward peace. Give all for all;
ask for nothing; require back nothing; abide purely
and unhesitatingly in me, and thou shalt possess me;
thou shalt be free in heart, and darkness shall not
tread thee down. Let this be thine endeavor, this thy
prayer, this thy desire: that thou mayest be stripped
of all selfishness, and naked follow the naked Jesus;
mayest die to thyself, and live eternally to me."

Thomas à Kempis

Those who live with the life of Christ, and share his
sacrifice, are those who bring the true meaning into
the daisies, and its joy into the lark's song; they are
the people who make the world young wherever they
live and die.

Fr. George Congreve

CHAPTER FIVE

The Path to Power

IT IS A COMMON EXPERIENCE among those who have entered into newness of life through the gate of prayer that, after the first rush of joyful wonder as the soul looks out upon a world of unguessed beauty, a sense of disappointment gathers and grows. It is not that we doubt the reality of the life divinely imparted: it is that we are surprised at its feebleness. In the first flush of joy we seemed to possess the strength of those that wait upon the Lord. We mounted up with wings as eagles; we ran all day long and were not weary. With our surrender to God, power seemed to pour into our soul; we seemed charged with creative potency; the wonder that had been wrought within us seemed to possess a magic, self-reproducing quality. For a brief space we saw ourselves sharing the wonderful spiritual fecundity of the great saints who enriched the church again and again with "new families." Some faint reflection of the productivity of a St. Francis or a Catherine Booth had been given us; wherever we went we found spiritual friends; in every eye we seemed to meet a response to our unspoken appeal.

But soon the glory faded. We could no longer fly or run;

we could not even walk without growing faint. Where once there had been rivers of living water, there was now but a faint trickle. Prayer, once so potently creative, could barely sustain the new man it had brought into being, and day by day the life whose beginnings had been so wonderful became weak and pulseless.

Doubts as to the completeness of our surrender suggested themselves, and far more destructive doubts as to the validity of the law of surrender arose. Were we not, after all, deceived by a religious catchword? Did anything really happen simply because we said, "Lord, I give myself to you, utterly and forever"? Is not this doctrine of the yielded self as mechanical as any of the shortcuts to salvation that are the stock-in-trade of itinerant evangelists? And if we were saved from capitulating to such doubt, it was only by the irrefutable fact that the little flame of life continued to burn within us—flickering, feeble, intermittent, but impossible to explain away. In the end we resigned ourselves to a mere spiritual existence. The flame, we argued, must remain dim and wind-blown in a world that is at war with God. Only exceptional souls need expect to be powerfully and influentially alive where everything conspires to crush and annihilate.

But such resignation, once we face issues squarely, is intolerable to an honest mind. To say that prayer which begins as a channel of creative power must continue and end as something that barely keeps us alive and no more, is to give away the whole case. If an act of devotion opened our soul's floodgates to the inrush of God's creative energy, shall a life of devotion do less? Must it not rather involve the cumulative force of a succession of such acts, and a succession so close as to make of all life a habit of surrender as continuous and inevitable as breathing?

If our life is feeble and impotent, it can be so only from

one of two causes: either we do not yet understand the law of surrender in its application to daily living, or, understanding it, we have failed to apply it. There is no room for a third alternative. God does not despise the weak—"He gives power to the faint, and to them that have no might he increases strength"—but he does not create weaklings. To revert to the language of the mystics, God wills that the holy Child that is born in the Bethlehem of the surrendered soul should grow into the fullness of stature of the man Christ Jesus. "O Jesus Christ, grow in me" is a prayer that cannot fail to be fulfilled.

What, then, would keep us from understanding the law of surrender and applying it to our daily lives? What else but self-love? One of the Fathers of the Desert once compared the love of praise to an onion. When stripped of one skin it is found to be sheathed in another, and as often as you strip it, you will find it still protected. The same might be said of self-love. It is not enough to put it to death once by a definite act of self-surrender; it must be put to death daily. Beneath each sheath of self-regard and vainglory there is another; and if we think that the soul can be stripped of it once and for all, we have still to learn the very elements of the spiritual life.

There is no magic word of surrender that will annihilate self-seeking. One true act of surrender is sufficient to dethrone self, but the dethroned king becomes the murderous conspirator. Nothing short of a life's discipline, a daily dying to self, not in pious imagination but by a succession of stern, practical acts of self-denial, will rout the enemy. Until we have begun to understand this and to turn it into practice, we have not set foot upon the path to power.

But here, at the very outset, we are met by a series of deep-rooted objections. Does this not spell asceticism, and will asceticism not betray us into a legalistic habit of life entirely alien to the free spirit of the gospel? Can anyone by taking thought add a cubit to his stature? Was it not said of old that he who is committed to God shall grow as the lily? Is not legitimate self-expression a far truer worship than self-mortification? Are we not meant to develop our impulses rightly rather than to mortify them?

I
THE NECESSITY OF SELF-DISCIPLINE

Volumes have been written concerning the legitimacy or otherwise of an ascetic element in Christianity, and very little of all that has been advanced on both sides of the question carries conviction to the average practical person, who is not in the position to trace the roots and estimate the historical value of the two rival ideals—the ascetic and the humanist. To most, asceticism resolves itself into monasticism. Poverty, celibacy, and obedience to a human superior are its sum and substance. Even where the application of the ascetic principle to one's everyday life in the world is admitted, the very word conjures up forbidding visions of a body emaciated by much fasting and weakened by self-inflicted chastisement.

Over and against such a conception, the ideal of a Christian life that appeals to our deepest nature is that which develops spontaneously, opening itself to God like a flower drawing sustenance, not from external mechanisms, but from the hidden sap of the spiritual soil, drinking in freshness and power as the lily drinks the dew. Fastings, vigils, and the hair shirt are poor and meretricious stage properties beside the healing, health-giving, invigorating influences that pass straight from the bosom of God into the expectant, aspiring soul. Life has but one law, after all—friendship with God. Let a soul live with God, and it will hate everything that is mean and vile. Let it look on the beauty of God, and it too will become beautiful. Let it love God, and "the expulsive power of a new affection" will do what a lifetime of self-torture cannot do. St. Augustine spoke well when he said, "Love, and do what you like."

That the soul that lives with God, and lives in God, will be transformed into that same image from glory to glory, is, of course, splendidly true; but, as a matter of hard fact, it is precisely that intimate transforming union with God that is for most of us impossible until, by steady self-discipline, we have cleared away the hindrances to such union. This does not mean that we must wait for union with God until all that hinders it is cleared away by dint of laborious effort, but that we must in union with God mortify our members for the perfecting of that union.

There are elect souls whose growth is as that of the lily, and they are of the *grand race*; but the majority of people who insist that the spiritual life must be of the lily order are unfortunately themselves far more like thistles than lilies. One cannot, for instance, take part in church life without being struck by the personal touchiness and ambition of many church workers; in nearly every case the petty self-seeking that is the scandal of religious life is most accentuated (as, indeed, one would expect it to be) in those who most vehemently insist that the Christian life is not an affair of rule or method, but a free, spontaneous response to a spiritual environment—a response as natural as breathing. They seem pathetically unaware that their theory has so little worked in their own case that they have not even succeeded in eliminating self-interest in holy things, let alone in everyday life.

But we still must answer the objection that even if it is a fact that self-discipline is an essential condition of true self-realization, and something in us has got to die before we can achieve fullness of life, it still remains true that the Christian's quarrel is with sin, and not with the innocent natural human impulse; he is certainly called to mortification, but it is his sins, not his nature, that he must mortify. This argument would hold water if "sin" were something extraneous to our nature, something obtruded upon the unwilling soul. But while we may hypostatize sin for convenience in argument, it is quite otherwise when we come to deal with it in actual life.

For practical purposes it is impossible to separate sin from the natural impulses through which it manifests itself, and into the fiber of which it insinuates itself. We cannot, for instance, say, "I will kill my ignoble deference to the opinion of others," without saying in the same breath, "I will mortify that perfectly natural and innocent love of approbation which is part of my makeup." We cannot fight against sins of the tongue without doing violence to that, in itself, quite harmless talkativeness which gives these sins a chance. We cannot master the lusts of the flesh without dealing sternly with the body which is their instrument. We cannot combat pride without humbling and chastening our natural self-esteem.

No artificial distinction between fighting against sin and mortifying our natures will stand, once we get down to the bedrock of reality. There is none so spiritual, or so devoted to God's service, as not to need constant mortification, lest having preached to others, he himself become a castaway.

Due to a popular misinterpretation of the spirit and purpose of Christian asceticism, resulting from the often deplorable excesses of individual ascetics, we have come to identify it with stoic indifference and Pharisaic gloom. Nothing could be further from the truth. The Stoic endures hardships and wrongs without wincing because he believes that nothing can really hurt him; he feels himself superior to all that fate may bring or human beings can do to him. The Christian ascetic knows nothing of such proud superiority. He serves a Master whose heart was pierced with the scorn and ingratitude of humanity; and his union with the Man of Sorrows, far from making him indifferent, makes him more keenly sensitive both to joy and to pain.

His active austerities spring from a passion to enter into the sufferings of Christ; his passive endurance is the fruit of his union with Christ, who, when he was reviled, reviled not again. Nor is his asceticism productive of gloom. He mortifies himself not that he may kill the joy that is within him, but that he may lift that joy above the plane of sense and fix it beyond the reach of circumstance and mood. The natural man is joyful at the wedding-feast; the mortified man is as joyful in loneliness and unrequited toil, for he has learned to turn sorrow into joy, and his joy no man takes from him.

The way to life is, of necessity, a strait and narrow way, and there are many rough places and lonely valleys awaiting the pilgrim. But it is doubly hard (though we are slow to believe it) for those who have not learned the royal secret of mortification. Our habitual misuse of words has led us to imagine that Christian freedom gives us the liberty to follow the mood and impulse of the moment, and we protest against anything that would put fetters upon this liberty. Spontaneity, we say, means joyousness, and joy is the very essence of Christianity. Yet, when we go below the surface, we cannot disguise from ourselves that our cult of spontaneity and freedom has brought us no increase of joy. Quite on the contrary, our religious life is pitched in the minor key, and our public worship, where it is not frigidly formal, is marked by wistfulness and pathos rather than by joyfulness.

When we take the trouble to sit down and study the

lives of some of those ascetics whose gloominess we took for granted, we find behind their austerities a sheer contagious gladness that gives our theories an uncomfortable shaking. The radiant face of Blessed Angela of Foligno, glowing like a rose and lit up with eyes like candles; the shrewd, blithe humor of St. Teresa; the exuberant mirth of that peculiar old monk, St. Paul of the Cross; the quiet happiness of St. Benedict and his followers, especially that freest of souls, St. Gertrude; the engaging *bonhomie* and unfailing gaiety of St. Philip Neri; the magic joy of St. Francis—how they haunt us as we ponder them! Do what we like, the merry laughter of these little servants of Christ cuts through our preconceived notions about liberty of soul and makes our so-called spontaneity appear as slavery.

And slavery indeed it is. True spontaneousness is the fruit of discipline. The artist who has mastered the technique of his art through self-discipline is the one who can best respond to the vision and inspiration of the moment. How many painters have failed to express their vision because the energy that ought to have gone to its recording was spent in a vain struggle with an imperfectly mastered medium! How many poets and writers lose their most sublime inspirations in their search for the luminous phrase, the revealing word! It is the same in the art of life.

If we would single out one thing above any other that blights our spiritual life with sadness, it is our sheer futility. We futilely perceive our vocation, because we cannot bend our intelligence and our wills to our vision. A crisis calls us, but our moral and spiritual fiber is too slack, and we futilely turn from its stern demands. A stirring message thrills us with new joy and hope, but our vagrant moods quench the newfound light, and we pay for our golden moment with long, leaden hours of futile reaction. If we deal faithfully with ourselves, we shall come to the conclusion that our futility is rooted in disobedience and self-indulgence. During the World War many a man who had lived comfortably and at ease and had found life a dreary, ineffectual business, suddenly discovered a well of joy and power in himself, once he endured the hard discipline of the training camp and the battlefield. And we may experience the same change in our spiritual life, if we would only discard our dilettante conception of freedom and go into the trenches with Christ.

There is among us an unhealthy cult of life which militates against the ideal of discipline. In our anxiety to lay due emphasis upon the positive, constructive character of Christianity, we have made a shibboleth of its doctrine of free, abundant, overflowing life, complete with splendid vigor and inalienable gladness. There is far too much talk about life and living to be healthy, far too much of deliberate and self-conscious cultivation of vitality to be safe. Yet, as one watches certain impassioned apostles of life, one is not impressed by their own vital quality. Far from reproducing the strong, steady, triumphant life of their Master, their energy seems to exhaust itself in a somewhat flamboyant and hectic paraphrase of certain elements in his teaching; and too often they exhibit a flabby, loafing, feverish habit which suggests a very low vitality indeed.

There is nothing to be surprised at in this, since he who seeks his own life shall lose it. We must at all costs recover the splendid spiritual courage that turns its back on life, that puts self beneath its feet. That royal habit of soul might conceivably be created and sustained without daily discipline and mortification; but if so, we have no record of such an achievement in all the annals of sanctity. One imagines that few would care to maintain that their own lives are the brilliant exception to this rule!

And if life is one key word of the present age, love is another. We claim to have discovered "the greatest thing in the world" as none of our forefathers did, to have gained an insight into the hidden beauties and delicacies of love which past generations lacked. We define our faith in terms of love, and we reduce all mortality to love. But with all our new-born sensitiveness and delicacy of perception, our love lacks largeness and fixity. It is an emotion rather than a principle. It makes sympathetic, highly strung personalities of us; it does not make us persons who are as a hiding-place from the wind and a covert from the tempest. It begets in us a restless passion for service; it does not breed an unalterable sense of vocation. It quickens our imaginative insight into the lives of others; it does not lead us to identify ourselves with the common life of our brethren in such a way that we share not so much their sorrows and failures, but the atoning sorrow, sacrifice, and victory of our common Savior.

Again the key to the problem is discipline. Love, as Thomas à Kempis reminds us, is not merely an exaltation, a joy, a thrilling experience; it is essentially and fundamentally "circumspect, humble and upright, not yielding to softness or to lightness, not attending to vain things; it is sober, chaste, firm, quiet and guarded in all the senses." In the last resort, both love and life resolve themselves into *spiritual staying power*. And there is no spiritual staying power without lifelong, unrelenting discipline.

II
The Master Move of Christian Asceticism

Try as we may, we cannot escape from the ascetic principle in Christian living—a principle, as someone has remarked, "as deeply seated in human nature as domesticity itself." This does not mean, of course, that all asceticism is Christian, or that Christianity can be exhausted in terms of asceticism. Much of the asceticism practiced within the Catholic church has been utterly unchristian and has served to obscure the light of the gospel for many generations. All attempts, whether Catholic or Protestant, to make Christianity a religion of self-repression, end by opening the door to license. Nature is a stickler for her rights, and she takes terrible revenge upon those who attempt to deny them.

But we need stand in no danger of mistaking the false asceticism for the true. Christian asceticism is always distinguished by two guiding marks: *its motive is not a desire to acquire superior merit, or to achieve self-improvement, but an impulse of pure love; and it begins, not with the body, but with the spirit.*

It is by its motive that Christian asceticism is lifted out of the region of gloom and becomes a minister of gladness. Mortification engaged in with a view to self-culture and self-improvement, as the athlete endures hardness that he may excel in the race, is always a dreary affair. It certainly produces strength, but it is a pagan strength, with the seeds of decay in its heart. For mortification which begins in self-regard must perforce end in self-righteousness—that gloomy decadence of the strenuous soul.

But Christian mortification is rooted in selfless devotion. The Christian soul longs to endure hardness, to toil, to suffer, to deny itself to the death, not for purposes of spiritual self-aggrandizement, but out of a consuming desire to share the labors and sufferings of the One who submitted himself to the limitations and disciplines of a poor man's life for our sakes. It was the passion to be brought into fuller sympathy and closer union with the Man of Sorrows that made St. Teresa cry out, "Let me suffer, or not live!" *No mortification can be called fully Christian which is not an authentic, irrepressible movement of love.* And such mortification will leave its impression upon our prayer life. One act of self-denial with the master-motive of love behind it can transform our praying from the beating of the empty air into the power that removes mountains. There is only one secret of prevailing prayer—the love that crucifies self and enthrones God in a lifelong series of definite acts of love; and when we come to analyze these acts, we shall see that behind even the most spontaneous and positive of them is the practice of daily mortification.

This mortification has nothing in common with self-torture. Its goal is not the mutilation or suppression, let alone the extinction of the natural powers, but their right use in the service of love. It aims not for death, but for life. Its spirit is positive and constructive. If, for instance, we mortify our tongue, it is not that we may reduce it to silence, but that we may fit it to speak good tidings of great joy. Suddenly—after months of severe restraint, perhaps—we find ourselves able to speak words that make dull eyes to shine and hard hearts to yield. We know now why we had to keep silence so long. Before we put the bridle on our tongues, our words were idle and impotent; now they are charged with vital power. And the keeping of silence and the going forth into speech are twin movements of the same love. It was the love that burns to fit ourselves for the Master's use that prompted the silence; it was the love that yields all faculties to God so that he might use them which inspired the utterance. And love is pure joy.

Christian mortification is not a dreary penance. Its restraints are radiant with promise and hope; its austerities are the luxuries of the heart that loves. The truly self-disciplined soul has all the attractiveness of one who is ruled by love. Self-regarding asceticism develops the stronger but less lovely traits of a person's character; Christian mortification is a soil in which sweetness and natural virtues spring up like flowers. As we have said already, the Christian ascetic has always attracted people by his sheer gaiety of heart, a gaiety as contagious as children's laughter.

It is the motive of Christian asceticism that confers authority upon it. "Christ's whole life was a cross," says Thomas à Kempis, "and do you seek rest and joy for yourself?" We cannot read the life of our Lord with unprejudiced vision without realizing that he trod the path of daily self-denial, in small things as well as great, that indeed "his life is our way." When we remember that he once fasted for forty days and often spent long, cold nights in prayer, we are only touching the outermost fringe of his devotion. When we realize that he endured insults and bitter scorn in perfect meekness, we are only laying our finger on certain striking symptoms of a deep-rooted habit. It is as we study his methods as a teacher, his bearing as a healer, his conduct as a friend, his wisdom as a leader, his skill as a seeker of the lost, that we gain any degree of insight into the depth and completeness of his self-abnegation, his unreserved self-surrender, his divine humility.

"Measure all by the cross," says Robertson of Brighton. "Do you want success? The cross was failure. Do you want a name? The cross is infamy. Is it to be cheerful and happy that you live? The cross is pain and sharpness. Do you live that the will of God may be done in you and by you in life and death? Then, and only then, the spirit of the cross is in you. When once a man has learned that, the power of the world is gone; and no man need bid him, in denunciation or in invitation, not to love the world." Jesus lived supremely in the spirit of the cross, and it is the cross—not merely the historic cross upon Calvary, but the cross in the heart of

God, the principle of sacrifice which lies at the foundation of the universe—that gives its justification and its power to Christian asceticism. We sometimes forget that the way of the cross is not only the way of the Savior to the soul of humanity, and the ultimate path of the cosmos itself to its destiny; it is also the soul's way to God. To let Jesus bear the cross alone is the most deadly way of making that cross of no effect.

We are now in the position to see the bearing of self-discipline and mortification upon prayer. Mortification, insofar as it is truly Christian, is nothing else than "the practice of the cross." The spirit of the cross is the soul of true prayer, for, as we have seen, prayer is fundamentally an act of self-giving. We cannot really know the nature and the power of prayer until we know something of what it means to be crucified with Christ. The soul that is not united to the Crucified cannot give itself in prayer.

Bunyan and most, if not all, of the great Puritan and Evangelical theologians have regrettably limited the scope of the cross in human life. In *The Pilgrim's Progress* the cross is introduced near the beginning of Christian's journey, as the place where the burden of sin rolls off the pilgrim's back and is seen no more. It is mentioned at later stages merely as the ground of the sinner's confidence and his refuge in times of distrust or relapse. But the power of the cross is not thus to be confined. It is rather the controlling principle of our new life in God from beginning to end—its revealing light as well as its consuming fire, the secret of its beauty as well as the source of its strength.

And those who pray most potently in the spirit of the cross are not those to whom prayer comes easily. The soul that has what is commonly called "a gift of prayer," and finds no difficulty in passing a whole hour perhaps in eloquent and even rapturous devotion, is a soul that needs to take grave heed to itself. Prayer that has a vital background and is a fit channel of power is always a hard and humiliating business. Its strength resides, not in its freedom, but in its limitations; not in its exuberance, but in its restraints. We sometimes plead that we are temperamentally unfitted for the life of prayer; and it may well be that our natural disposition and make-up are incompatible with one type of devotion or another. But the prayer that we have defined as creative is not a matter of temperament at all. What hinders us from achieving it is simply our share in the common human disinclination to face reality, and in the common human fear of the cross. Once we are willing to take up the cross and follow Jesus, we have already begun to pray.

And it is because the motive behind the true prayer life is symbolized by the cross of Christ that the disciple is preserved from that consciousness of sacrifice which defaces so much human goodness. The determining impulse behind the cross was not sacrifice but obedience. We say that Jesus chose the path that led to Calvary; it is even truer to say that the only path he chose was the path of obedience, and had that path led him to a king's throne, he would still have chosen it. Romantic heroism would cry, "Lo, I have come to save the world by the bitter death of the cross." Divine obedience said, "Lo, I come to do thy will, O God."

III
THE REAL ARENA OF OUR WARFARE

We now come to the second fundamental characteristic of Christian mortification: *it must not begin with the body, but with the spirit*. To reverse this order is to fall into externalism. That most scantily appreciated of all the Collects in the Anglican Prayer Book—the Collect for the Feast of the Circumcision—might well serve as the motto of those who desire to find the true path to power. In dry, sober, weighty fashion, it enunciates the whole Christian philosophy of mortification: "Almighty God, who madest thy Son to be circumcised, and obedient to the law for man: Grant us the true circumcision of the spirit, that our hearts and all our members being mortified from all worldly and carnal lusts, we may in all things obey thy blessed will."

With all our polemic against externalism in religion and our emphasis upon its spiritual character, we are very slow to learn that the strategic center of our spiritual warfare is not the body with its appetites, or the mind with its ambitions, but the spirit itself. That is why our progress in the Christian life is often so disappointing. We offer ourselves to God, renouncing material self-indulgence and worldly ambition. We keep a watchful eye over our physical and mental activities, striving to yield all our members as instruments of righteousness. And yet we fail. Our lives are reformed, but, on the whole, impotent. Our Christianity is undoubtedly there, but it does not shine, does not radiate. Our prayers comfort us in trouble and support us in our struggle, but they lack dynamic. They do not create new situations; they do not even transform old situations, but only make them tolerable. Presently we find ourselves suffering from spiritual lassitude and emptiness of spirit. We groan under a weariness that is worse than failure. It is not that our spiritual life does not work, but that it works as indifferently as our smoke-laden lungs, our ill-organized business, our wobbly political machine, our haphazard system of education. It is not the miracle of and glory of our life; it is only one of its many mediocrities.

There is only one cure—to begin at the center. We have

sought to mortify our worldly ambition; what about our spiritual ambition? We have tried to regulate our domestic emotions; what about our religious emotions? One sometimes hears religious people lamenting the defections and failures of the church, and then adding, by way of consolation: "But there is so much genuine goodness, so much unconscious Christianity among people outside the churches, that really we need not be unduly depressed about the religious situation." But that is to take an entirely superficial view of the matter. If there is a vast amount of unrecognized and often unconscious Christianity in England today, it is ultimately derived, if not from the organized churches (a matter which is open to discussion), then most assuredly from that which the churches have produced and conserved throughout the centuries. It is from the society of the redeemed that redemptive influences radiate; it is through his body, however sorely wounded and maimed, that Christ is seeking to manifest himself to the world. And if that body be indeed sick unto death, the world must ultimately suffer a loss that is all the more tragic the less it is recognized.

The iron in the blood of the nation was put there by the church of the Puritans; the sweetness of domestic religion, which gives tenderness and purity to homes where the name of Christ is never mentioned, sprang from the genius of Anglicanism. And if the House of God becomes a den of thieves, what can we expect from the city; if the priest profanes the altar, what hope is there for the people? The work of purging must begin in the sanctuary. It is the money-changers in the temple that are the menace, not the money-grabbers outside. We need not fear that the world will be left in darkness, so long as the altar lights are kept burning.

This is unpopular doctrine, but it holds the key to life. The first step on the path to power, whether for churches or for individuals, is to curb spiritual ambition and to guard religious emotions with unceasing vigilance. If one were asked to single out the one weakness which, more than any other, has robbed both individual and corporate Christian life of power, it would have to be the unwillingness to endure self-denial which is so characteristic of our age. In the individual, the lack of discipline most often takes the shape of an unbridled surrender to the religious mood or emotion of the moment, and an unquestioning gratification of personal affinities, tastes, and ambitions. In corporate life this spirit of self-seeking often expresses itself in sensuous ritual without the safeguard of lofty doctrine or wholesome moral discipline, in a sensational revivalism which panders to the crude emotions, or in an ambitious intellectualism which flatters the dilettante understanding, but leaves the spiritual nature of man untouched.

Our private devotions and our public worship are alike shorn of power for lack of that stern and persistent discipline which is its natural background. It is as useless to expect creative prayer and dynamic worship to spring from an undisciplined habit of life which yields to every impulse and puts self-expression in the forefront, as it is to expect to gather grapes from thistles. Let us face the fact that we are at war with the forces of unbelief and sin, and that the first requisite for war is a trained soldiery. No amount of glowing emotion, flashing insight, and eagerness for action can make up for the lack of that iron in the soul that comes from enduring the hardness of the Christian soldier. In our churches are many well-meaning people, some of them exceedingly attractive in their eagerness to do good and their quick appreciation of everything high and lovely, who have never learned to say No to their natural impulses and inclinations—especially when these impulses and inclinations operate in the realm of religion—and who have never troubled to question their affinities or to sift their motives. The consequent powerlessness is the problem and the reproach of the church of Christ today.

It is profoundly symptomatic that many seek to account for that powerlessness by the dearth of great preachers and leaders. If you get a really strong personality in the pulpit, they say, you will not need to complain of empty and uninfluential churches. Nothing proves so strikingly the completeness of our obsession with human personality. We seek refuge from a weakness due to self-indulgence and self-seeking in the dominance of one great self—that of the preacher and leader. Such dominant personalities have their place, of course; but the power of the church lies not in the gathering of crowds round a compelling leader, but *in the spiritual force of the corporate body*—a body composed of disciplined, devoted members, bent on the pilgrimage from self to God.

Until we learn this lesson, and seek that circumcision of the spirit which brings every religious, as well as what we call secular, impulse into the captivity of Christ, our conferences and movements will leave us more powerless and more disillusioned than they found us. As individuals and as churches we are sent into the world, not to express our own views and conceptions of what the Christian life should be, but to manifest Christ—to live in the power and under the rule of the Incarnation. If we know anything about our Lord with certainty, it is, in the words of the Collect, that he was "obedient to the law for men." He, the radiantly holy, the triumphantly vital, the Lord of liberty who broke the fetters of man-made law, submitted himself to the law for the sake of his frail and sinful brethren. For their sakes he sanctified himself; for their sakes "He, being in the form of God, thought it not a thing to be snatched at to be equal with

God, but made himself of no reputation, and took upon himself the form of a servant."

And we are here to show him to the world; to continue, in our small measure, his divine self-emptying. But we are tainted by the spirit of a self-assertive age, impatient of restraint. We tend to look upon ourselves rather as free-lance adventurers than as servants. We like to think of ourselves as leaders, or as members of some brilliant and original group centered round a great leader. What self-discipline we exercise concerns itself almost exclusively with our lower promptings. We constantly forget that the spiritual realm is our supreme battleground, for the spiritual realm is not only the last refuge, but also the most impregnable fortress of self-will. So long as we fail to keep sentry there, we shall remain impotent.

IV
A GRADUAL TRANSFIGURATION

The question of bodily discipline should normally arise out of the question of spiritual discipline, and considered in its relation to the spiritual, it is not likely to betray us into sterile excesses. Two familiar truisms emerge at the very outset. On the one hand, bodily discipline cannot be ignored because body and spirit are inextricably intertwined; on the other hand, it should always be kept in a strictly subordinate place. Regarding the first point little needs to be said. The days when people looked upon the soul as an entity entirely independent of the body, which, for all spiritual purposes, might be conceived of as functioning a million miles away from the body, are past. Philosophy knows nothing of such an entity; and laboratory psychology has driven home the humiliating truth that a good dinner may transport the soul from spiritual wistfulness to gross complacency, and a grain of an Eastern drug exalt it to the realm of ecstatic vision or plunge it into the gloom of the vilest hells.

We cannot any longer preach a gospel of the spirit which ignores the body, but while we rightly emphasize the need for a redemption which includes the ill-housed, starved, stunted body of the slum-dweller as well as his soul, we are not so quick to insist that the person who fails to discipline his body, let alone the person who pampers it, has no hope of achieving spiritual strength and beauty.

It is at this point that much of our present-day preaching and teaching fails. Our social gospel is incomplete. It does not embrace the full Christian doctrine of the body. That individuals cannot rise to their spiritual destiny while living under degrading physical conditions is only one-half of the truth about the body, and—with all due respect to social workers—not the most important half. The other half of the truth is that no one who neglects bodily discipline—whether he is a well-paid artisan gorging himself with coarse food, or an aristocrat of culture choosing his refined physical plea- sures with artistic restraint—can enter the kingdom that God has prepared for him.

Discipline is not merely a matter of refraining from excess. As in the things of the spirit, so in the things of the body; Christian discipline means the uprooting of self-grati- fication and self-will. The refined person who elects to have simple meals and simple clothing, but who chooses each course and each garment with no other thought than his own health, taste, and predilections, is as undisciplined, and as really given over to the flesh, as the gourmand and the luxuriously arrayed.

Our modern cult of health has lured many a lazy, self- indulgent individual into the hard path of physical disci- pline; but, as that remarkable woman, Miss Honnor

Morten, discerned many years ago, it has not encouraged a revival of physical discipline for spiritual ends:

> Brother Ass is entirely in the ascendant just now. Everyone is considering the body and how it ought to be dieted and how exercised, and the doctor is a far greater autocrat than the priest ever was; so that to bid for pleasures and rewards that are not bodily is not popular. The modern man diets to get "uric acid" out of his system, the monk of old dieted in order to get strength into his soul; the modern woman gets up early, not in order to seek the Holy Spirit by prayer, but to do breathing exercises to give capacity to her lungs. And the quaintest thing to the looker-on at these ridiculous rites is that their devotees are so weak and so miserable; whereas, when Brother Ass is treated to a little wholesome neglect, he generally becomes a contented and obedient animal.[8]

It is futile for us to point to the old monks and dilate upon the uselessness of their ascetic excesses, or to quote the warning by St. Paul against a religion of "Touch not, taste not, handle not." We do not need to be told that a fierce and savage asceticism is as much governed by self-will as a course of luxury, and that nature avenges all such outrages upon her sanctity. We need not lay special emphasis upon the fact that to draw any undue attention to the body, by means of inflicting discomfort or pain upon it, is not to mortify but to pamper the flesh. All this we know already, and since excessive mortification is not a sin to which our age is in the least addicted, the situation does not call for a polemic against undue asceticism.

[8] *Things More Excellent*, p. 38.

What we have to concern ourselves with is not whether the monks were wise or otherwise in their treatment of the body, but what we ourselves, living in our time, propose to do about "Brother Ass." How are we going to yoke our bodies to the redemptive purpose of the Kingdom? How are we going to make them worthy of him who transfigured our flesh into the likeness of the Eternal by taking upon himself the form of a servant, and living the hard, frugal life of a poor working-man in an oppressed land?

Here is the crux of the matter. We believe in physical mortification, not because we esteem the body as vile, but, on the contrary, because our faith in the Incarnation pledges us to a high conception of the body's sanctity and destiny. Mortification is not the sacrificing of the body to the alleged interests of the soul; it is the expression of the soul's regard for the body as an instrument of holiness. The body is meant to be not the mere outer garmenting, but the palpitant medium of the soul—to take on its mold, and to glow with its splendor. It is destined itself to become spiritual, not by means of an emptying process, as a false asceticism would have us believe, but by a gradual transfiguration in which no natural endowment is lost.

It is possible for a person to become radiantly and triumphantly Christian under the most hostile circumstances and in the most degrading environment. If we are tempted to doubt that, we need only to remind ourselves that many of the early Christians were slaves and to recall what Roman slavery meant. But it is *not* possible for a person to enter into his full Christian birthright without severe discipline of body as well as of spirit. A person's environment may be ideal, and every circumstance conspire to further his highest development, but if he imagines that he can achieve his spiritual destiny with a slack-fibered, capricious, pampered body, he is laboring under a tragic delusion. More spiritual failure—especially failure in prayer—than we like to think can be traced to bodily slackness.

The question as to the wisdom of *voluntary* mortification troubles many earnest souls, and in most cases the difficulty arises out of a misuse of the term "voluntary." To practice voluntary mortification does not mean to go out of one's way to invent mortifications for the sake of achieving ascetic perfection. To do this is simply to follow the promptings of self-will, and a self-willed mortification is a contradiction in terms. But there is such a thing as mortification, self-imposed, indeed, but imposed upon oneself in obedience to a genuine inward spiritual demand; such mortification is as truly "from God" as a reversal of fortune or the loss of reputation. Only the fanatical and unbalanced would deny that it is a right instinct, and not sterile eccentricity, for one surrounded by the temptations of wealth to cultivate simplicity of life; or for another, who lives among the beauties of a quiet countryside, to spend some time each year at a slum settlement, in order to kill his pagan shrinking from contact with ugliness.

Both are "self-chosen" or "voluntary" mortifications, yet one would think as little of condemning them as of saying that the parents of an only child are wrong in seeking companions for it, since God evidently means it to be alone. So far from being wrong, it is a matter of sheer common sense that a person whose circumstances afford no opportunities for enduring the hardness of the Christian soldier should seek such opportunities for himself, provided always that they be sought along sane lines, involving no neglect of common duty and chosen in humble dependence upon the leading of God, who works through our choices as well as through circumstances.

V

OUR GREAT NEED: A DISENTANGLED HEART

"You have yet many things to part with," says Thomas à Kempis to the aspiring soul; and those who have set themselves wholeheartedly upon the path that leads from self to God will sooner or later be confronted with the demand for renunciation. The demand may come in the line of everyday activity, leaving us free to follow our accustomed mode of living, but with a new spirit of self-denial. Or it may come, as it did to St. Francis, as a call to renounce things wholly lawful in themselves and to follow Christ in the way of literal poverty and self-stripping—"naked to follow the naked Jesus," to use the bald phrase of *The Imitation*.

It has been the habit of Protestant piety to deny the validity of these particular and purely individual vocations and to insist upon one way of discipleship for all. But Christ himself sanctioned such special vocations, and enjoined upon those who did not have them to put no hindrance in the way of their brethren who felt themselves called in such ways. "He that is able to receive it, let him receive it" was our Lord's ruling regarding such as "made themselves eunuchs for the Kingdom of Heaven's sake."

As to voluntary poverty, there have always been sincere and thoughtful souls who, realizing the futility and slavery of superfluous possessions, have turned to Lady Poverty for emancipation and enlargement. Today, when the ordeal of war has proved so much of our gold to be but dross, not a few of those who once insisted that a comfortable income and luxurious surroundings were essential to the production of good work, are realizing that what they thought the hallmark of high culture was in reality the evidence of a vulgarized taste. Once more people are casting behind them what seemed to them to make life fine and free, and in doing so discover that they are merely discarding a hampering load of rubbish. They are coming to see that Jesus was right when he taught that it is only by letting go of the "clutter" of life that we can grasp its true treasure. Renunciation, instead of being decried as part of a subterranean conspiracy against life, is coming to be recognized as the key to humanity's true kingdom, the gate into life's treasure-house.

But excellent as this is, the Christian call to poverty in its fullest sense is based upon other considerations. That call, which is coming to increasing numbers today, is not so much a challenge to discover the secret of true wealth as a constraint to share with Christ the hard, common life of our poor brethren. Christian poverty—or, to rehabilitate the old phrase, Evangelical poverty—certainly holds within itself the secret of true wealth and happiness, but its motive, like that of all Christian renunciation, is the heart's desire to share our Lord's self-emptying. It is this motive that determines the character of the vocation to literal poverty—a vocation as definite and individual as the vocation of a foreign missionary or a minister of the gospel. It takes its rise not from any philosophy of wealth, or from any theory of ownership, but from the love that longs to give itself and to sacrifice itself to the uttermost.

There is, of course, such a thing as the deliberate choice of poverty from a conviction that wealth, or possession in any shape, is part of a godless system, and such a vocation may be essentially Christian in its nature. But the call to Evangelical poverty in the specific sense is something entirely distinct from any social theory. It is the response of the loving heart to the demand of Christ to "sell all" and follow him. It is the embodiment of the soul's desire to be wholly identified with him who "emptied himself of all but love." It is the vocation of those who offer themselves to God that they might express in their

persons the poverty of Christ and so become living sacra-
ments, as it were, of the Incarnation.

Those who are thus called rejoice in sharing the common
life of the poor. They do not frown on earthly possessions or
decry the good things of material life. They choose poverty, not
because they think it meritorious or good in itself, but
because they believe that by renouncing legitimate comfort
and being poor with Christ, they are hastening the day when
disabling poverty shall be wiped off the face of the earth and
all shall share in God's good gifts. They are poor that they
may make many rich. They turn their backs upon the refine-
ments and luxuries enjoyed now by the few that they might
secure the really fine and gladdening things of life for all of
humanity. Their poverty is not the cult of the simple life, nor
an aesthetic or philosophic experiment; it is the holy, unpre-
tentious poverty of the carpenter's shop at Nazareth, and of
the divine Wayfarer who had no place to lay his head. It
lacks the dirt and the unnecessary physical torture of
medieval religious poverty, but it is as real, as untheatrical,
and as joyous as that of St. Francis.

One feels convinced that this call to poverty, as expressive
of the self-emptying of the Redeemer, is heard by not a few
today—heard, but not responded to—and that the reason why
the mass of our prayer is so feeble and futile is that we allow
religious prejudice and self-regarding considerations to keep us
from making renunciations to which we know ourselves called,
but which would make us unpopular in the religious world.[9]

The world is waiting for souls who are wholly detached
from earthly considerations and wholly attached to God. It
is for want of complete detachment—the necessary condition of whole-hearted attachment—that our faith remains
dim and our prayer feeble. It was a common saying among
the Fathers of the Desert that if a man took more thought for

his life than was necessary to keep him alive, he was not fit for the highest type of prayer. We are now discovering how right their instinct was.

Looking back over the curious inefficiency of so much in recent religious effort, which was born of a genuine vision but lacked staying power, and looking back also upon one's personal prayer life, which mirrors the age in so many ways, one realizes as never before the truth of Lacordaire's dictum that the first foundation of any valid spiritual work is *a detached heart*. Nothing can make up for the lack of a disentangled heart; spiritual vision and insight, moral earnestness, religious genius are futile, so long as the heart remains attached to earthly comforts and allurements.

Since it is the pride of possession which, more than anything else, lays the heart of the age in iron chains of servitude, it is not at all surprising that there should come to some aspiring souls the call to make the extreme renunciation—to empty themselves of all possessions, to renounce all claim to be reckoned among the "better" classes. We long to recall a Christless world and a weakened church to eternal values, to persuade Christian souls especially to turn from the temptations of mammon and the tyranny of false social standards and unchristian distinctions, and to realize their brotherhood in Christ and their citizenship in the Kingdom of God.

[9]It is significant to find that so uncompromising a Protestant as Principal Denney was alive to the evil of our popular disparagement of anything like special vocations, and particularly special renunciations:

"I have an impression that a great deal of what is called 'interest' in the church is artificial, and that when it comes to the point of doing anything it is exceedingly difficult to get it done. The Protestant church has perhaps taught too exclusively the duty of consecrating to God the life we are born into, and left too little room for the truth that in this present evil world there must be great renunciations as well, if there are to be great Christian careers"—(*Letters of Principal James Denney to W. Robertson Nicoll*, p. 156).

But who is sufficient for these things? Is it not a task that might well fill a saint with misgiving? On the other hand, might it not be that for some of us who have seen the vision of the Kingdom of God, the only way of making our brethren see it also is by taking the extreme position—by becoming poor that we might inspire them to be rich as faithful stewards of God? Might it not be that at the root of our weakness in prayer and of our lurking doubt as to the efficacy of prayer, there lies this unanswered call, this unobeyed vision? Is it not possible that the disquieting spiritual ebb-tide of today is due to the fact that many of us have refused a call to take the way of the Incarnation? Certain it is that if we would be spiritually powerful, we must take our Lord's path to power.

And that path, while it includes special calls and renunciations, is not a path for the few only. To limit it to "canonized saints" is to depart from the Christian ideal. "Called to be saints" is St. Paul's description of a company of undisciplined and erring pagan souls, in a city notorious for its malodorous reputation even in an age of licentious cities. And when one Greater than St. Paul called upon all men to follow him, his cry was, "If *any man* will come after me, let him deny himself, and take up his cross daily, and follow me." There is no distinction here between the heroic ascetic and the innocently "enjoying" soul.

And this gospel of "any man" needs to be preached at Geneva as much as in Rome. When we sing,

> All the vain things that charm me most,
> I sacrifice them to his blood,

is it not with the tacit assumption that this sacrifice has a reality for, let us say, the foreign missionary that it cannot have for the young girl in the choir; that, indeed, in her case it must needs remain a pious metaphor? True, we do not limit Christ's call to self-denial to official "saints," but we often do what is even more mischievous: we seek to universalize it by means of a double interpretation—a literal one for spiritual heroes, and an allegorization for those who are spiritually weak. We say, in effect, that the good lady who endures an attack of toothache patiently is fulfilling, in her way, the same divine demand which impels her neighbor to a life of unobtrusive self-denial and ceaseless service.

As if anticipating this modern perversion, the Evangelist records how Jesus on one occasion, seeing the multitude following him, turned, not to his disciples as at other times, but to the motley crowd of common folk, and said: "If any man comes to me, and hates not his father, and mother, and wife, and children, and brothers, and sisters, yes, and his own life also, he cannot be my disciple. And whosoever does not bear his cross, and come after me, cannot be my disciple. . . . Whosoever of you who does not forsake all that he has, he cannot be my disciple." And still that call comes to every individual, and remains the inexorable condition of discipleship.

> Christ's church is in need of apostles. But how much is needed before we can earn that name, what subordination of sense to spirit, what humble consciousness of failings, what calm intelligence, what burning faith, and above all, what glowing charity! We must become "another Christ" among men, like him bringing a message of peace, a doctrine of liberty through the truth. . . . It is my resolution to be an apostle of prayer, that high and fruitful form of action, the more secure because it is secret, and works with God for souls.
>
> *Elizabeth Leseur*

The relation of myself to those for whom I pray must forever be modified by the fact that it is not I alone who have to do with them, but God and I together. . . . My relations to men, to the world, to the devil, to the flesh, to success, to ambition, and in fact to all things, whether heavenly or earthly, are to be brought by prayer into subordination to God, to receive his mighty impress and his determinative touch before they have any being. Thus prayer becomes a living of the outer life in the inner sanctuary. The visible is brought into the sphere of the invisible. The praying man is in the line of the great consequences, and to him belong the secrets of the Lord.

G. Granger Fleming

CHAPTER SIX

The Apostolate of Prayer

THERE IS NO ASPECT of the prayer life about which controversy has spun so baffling a web as intercession. How can prayer benefit anyone beyond the person who prays? How can prayer on behalf of others be effectual without infringing upon their free will? Why should the sick person who happens to have praying friends stand a better chance of recovery than the equally deserving sick person who has no one to say a prayer on his behalf? If prayer admittedly cannot change natural law, why should we expect it to change the laws which govern the moral and intellectual nature of those we pray for? These and a host of other much-debated questions have wrapped the subject in an obscuring cloud of controversial dust, and not a few of the answers given by orthodox apologists for prayer serve only to render that cloud more dense.

Moreover, our inveterate habit of discussing things from the outside instead of seeking to discover their inherent laws has had a practical result which can only be described as disastrous. Whereas in former times intercession was looked upon as hard toil for strong men, it has come to be regarded by the majority of people as a nice, quiet occupation especially suitable for delicate persons and invalids. Comparatively few look upon it as part of a Christian's vocation.

As a matter of fact, we still tend to interpret prayer apart from its larger context, in spite of the undeniable gains that the modern attitude has brought us. Intercessory prayer cannot be interpreted in a vacuum; it presupposes a spiritual universe, a world of grace within which alone it finds its justification. So long as we interpret the world and our destiny merely in terms of science and philosophy, our faith in intercessory prayer must of necessity be at the mercy of the latest scientific or philosophical theory. But if we enter the world of grace—a world redeemed, recreated, and unified in Christ—intercession becomes the most convincing and luminous fact in the world, and every valid result of scientific and philosophical inquiry will ultimately contribute to its right interpretation.

We have seen that prayer is based upon the conception of God as fullness of love. Every real prayer is the soul's response to that love in an act of self-surrender. The life of prayer is the life of conversion—a gradual, progressive turning from self to God. Potentially and ideally, that conversion is accomplished in the first genuine act of surrender, whereby the soul disassociates itself from sin and enters into its right relation with Eternal Love; actually it involves a lifetime of successive and increasingly complete acts of self-donation, such acts being the expression of a habit of daily self-denial and daily integration into Christ. Prayer is thus essentially an "imitation" of Christ in his self-surrender to the Father, a yielding up of the self that it may be filled with the fullness of God, a losing of life that it may be found again in him.

But this passing from the life of the flesh to the life that is hid with Christ in God is no mere pious sentiment or vague mysticism. It means the identification of the whole personality—mind, will, and emotion—with the mind and will and heart of God. It means loyal citizenship in the Kingdom of Love and Grace. It means making Christ's interests our own. It means to learn to think with God, to have the mind of Christ, to see the world through his eyes, to share his passion to save and redeem. It has well been said that "the heart of Christ in the heart of the Christian is the vital center of practical Christianity, the living fountain of all its healing agencies." And that heart is formed in us by prayer. As the soul lies open to God, his thoughts enter into us, his life of Love takes possession of us. His activity becomes ours.

I

Intercessory Prayer: A Long and Arduous Pilgrimage

It is at this point that the soul is drawn to the prayer of intercession. It has now arrived at a degree of self-identification with the purposes of God which makes it essential to take an active share in realizing them. Prayer is seen as an apostolate—a means of making God known to others and of bringing them within the sphere of grace. We do not ask how our praying can influence other lives; we do not begin to wonder if preaching and teaching or acts of beneficence are not far more rational and effective means of doing good in the world than prayer. These arguments have weight only with someone who approaches prayer theoretically or who still regards it as merely a means of obtaining things from God where other means fail.

But we know what prayer has wrought in our own lives.

We know that it has been effectual in as far as it has centered in an act of self-committal to God and in a resolve to take up the cross and follow Jesus in his self-sacrificing love. And we feel that since Christ himself wrought out salvation for others by a life of obedience even to death on the cross, so we, being joined to him and living in union with him, can offer our prayers and the life behind our prayers on behalf of others.

Once we grasp the true nature of prayer, the difficulties that are so often urged against the practice of intercession are seen to be entirely irrelevant. Knowing all human life to be one; knowing ourselves to be vitally and indissolubly knit to our brethren in God; knowing that he sees humanity as living in relations of mutual interdependence united by their common response to Eternal Love, intercession becomes a vital necessity. We see our mutual interdependence broken because of the failure of so many to respond to the love of God and take their place in his family; and the love of Christ constrains us to take his way of reaching these estranged ones—the way of self-oblation on their behalf.

Now we are in the position to realize how utterly mistaken that view of intercession is which relegates it to the weak and inactive. When Christ saw the fields of the world white unto harvest, he said, not to a group of dreamy mystics or holy invalids but to the twelve sturdy men who were to carry his gospel to the ends of the earth: "Pray *ye* therefore the Lord of the harvest, that he would send forth laborers into his harvest." Before the commission to preach and teach comes the vocation to prayer. It is at once the preliminary testing and the final triumph of the true apostle. It not only accompanies apostleship from beginning to end, it is itself an apostleship.

The instinct of the church was right when it recognized intercession as a distinct vocation, demanding all a strong man's powers, giving scope to his whole personality, sufficing as a life work for some of the noblest spirits and the brightest intellects. Our present-day utilitarianism has driven that instinct underground, but it can never die. And the time is at hand when it will emerge once more, and elect souls in all the churches will feel themselves called to a life of intercession, and be honored by their brethren as having been divinely appointed to a life of the most intense and concentrated spiritual activity.

But while such a call necessarily comes to the few, all are meant to share in the apostolate of prayer. We need only glance through the letters of St. Paul to realize how large a part intercession played in the strenuous life of the itinerant apostle. Of our Lord himself it is recorded that he was so hard pressed with external activity that he had no leisure so much as to eat, yet he spent whole nights in prayer—a course which our modern anxiety for "Brother Ass" would condemn as regrettably imprudent. No amount of activity can excuse us from the duty of intercession, and any activity however spiritual it may seem that incapacitates us for intercession is to be viewed with grave suspicion.

One reason why the person who looks at prayer from the outside tends to exalt preaching and practical philanthropy above intercession is that he looks upon intercession from the point of view of those for whom it is offered. His sole object being to alleviate the sufferings and increase the happiness of those about whom he is anxious, the thought naturally occurs to him that an inspiring message or a deed of kindly help is by far the quicker and better way to reach them than "mere" prayer. After all, intercession is the expression of sympathy and the same sympathy may find more effectual expression in other directions.

But the true apostle of prayer has an entirely different point of departure. He starts not from his sense of the world's

need, however poignant that sense may be, but from his realization of the deeper sorrow and the more intense longing in
the heart of him who bids him to pray—and it is these, and
not merely his own necessarily fluctuating compassion for the
sorrows and wrongs of man, that drive him to prayer.

Man's pain and wrong are acutely felt by him but they
reach him through the heart of Christ. So closely is he identified with Christ that no sword can pierce his heart without
passing through Christ's own heart also. Moreover, he has so
truly entered into his Lord's world-wide longing that nothing short of intercession embracing the whole world can
content him. He has learned to think universally, not because
he has reasoned himself out of insularity, but because his
whole being is devoted to the Savior of the worlds in whom
all are made one, and who is the Desire of all nations.

As in personal prayers, the core of intercession is not
"asking things for others" but an offering of one's soul to
God that it may become a fit vehicle of his redeeming power.
"O thou divine Lover of souls," cries the apostle of prayers,
"make of me a true repairer of thy wrongs, a true channel of
thy grace. Let no selfish interest dull me to anything that
concerns thy honor. Give me an apostolic heart, world-wide
in its love for all men—yea, let thy love towards men be my
very pulse!" The motto of the true intercessor must ever be:
"For their sakes I sanctify myself."

It is as we trace the beginnings of apostolic intercession
that we shall best be able to grasp its nature and scope. As
we have already seen, prayer, in most cases, begins with personal petition. We ask benefits for ourselves and for those
we love. Then we come to realize that the power of prayer
lies not in the external benefit, or even in the mental and
spiritual reinforcement that comes to us through it, but in
our heart-communion with God.

A new love takes possession of us, a new relationship transfigures life, a new world dawns upon our unsealed eyes. We know that communion with God not only means mastery over life, but that it is life itself. And as we humbly press closer to the heart of God and read a little of its secret, it is gradually borne in upon us that only as we die to self-love shall we be able to take our true place within that heart of love. We see that prayer, far from being a gentle meditation or a sweet emotion, is a long and arduous pilgrimage from self to God. Indeed, it is not the pilgrimage of those who imagine that God can be reached by human effort, but the progress of souls that have been redeemed by Christ and now desire to be wholly found in him.

II

A NEW WAY OF LOOKING AT OTHERS

Very early in that pilgrimage we begin to include in our prayers others who are not near and dear to us, and that not from purely altruistic motives. We realize that our progress towards God depends very largely upon our fellows. We have friends who praise and indulge us, and sooner or later we recognize that their blind love is not helping us towards spiritual adulthood. We also have detractors and enemies who work us ill, and we find ourselves again and again overcome of their evil, instead of being able to overcome it with good.

And so, harried and beaten in our struggle, we turn to our divine Friend and Counselor and lay our case before him. We bring friend and foe into the circle of our prayers, and as we do this we find that the mere fact of bringing them into the presence of God changes their relation to us and ours to them. They are no longer merely human units to whose stimulus, whether for good or ill, we, as other human units, react. They are real or potential fellow citizens in the Kingdom of God, called by God to co-operate with him and with us in the work of redemption. Insofar as they are a hindrance to us, they oppose not merely our progress but the great purpose of God in which both they and we are embraced. We see them more and more as the object of God's solicitude. He is seeking to guide and mold them; and it is their resistance to *him* that is the most important factor in anything that may be wrong in their conduct towards us.

To lift them thus into the light of God changes our attitude towards them, and not only by way of making us more patient and forgiving. The change goes deeper and is of more virile fibre. It means that henceforth these friends and foes of ours will not find us as open to their influence as we were before. Praise will no longer unbalance our foolish minds; blame and injury will no longer sting us to weak self-defense and retaliation. Henceforth we see them in relation to God. There are no longer two but three in our thought of them— ourselves, they, and God; and of that trinity God is the controlling and regulative factor.

As we view them in him, their power to annoy or weaken us is seen to be controlled and modified by the overruling power of Love. We realize that in the hands of that Love both the misguided kindness of friends and the malicious opposition of foes may be turned into so many means of grace and opportunities of progress. It is part of the mystery of that divine alchemy[10] by which Jesus himself turned the dross of humanity's false friendship and malignant enmity into the

___

[10]Alchemy: The medieval chemical science and speculative philosophy whose aim was the transmutation of the base metals into gold. *(Webster's Third New International Dictionary)*

pure gold of perfect humanity and saviorhood. In that miraculous transmutation we are called to cooperate, and intercession is the philosopher's stone that turns the clay of human perversity into material for the perfecting not only of ourselves, but of the whole family of God. We learn to make capital of friend and foe alike; not, indeed, in using them as pawns in our game, but in so using their attitude and action towards us as to make them factors in our common redemption.

It is in the course of this extension of our prayer life to include those whose conduct seems to be a hindrance that we are, as a rule, first inspired with something of apostolic fervor. Through refusing to see either friend or foe apart from his true relation to God, we realize our mutual dependence and indissoluble brotherhood in God. And with that growing realization and the closer communion with God which it involves, we catch something of the divine sorrow for those of our brethren who have taken the wrong road.

Sometimes in a flash, sometimes gradually, we are touched with something of God's own passion to redeem. In one way or another, according to our varying natures and circumstances we are impelled to become his fellow-workers. We cry with St. Ignatius, "O my God, if men only knew thee, they would never sin!" and resolve to do what we can to make God better known among men. Whether by preaching and teaching, by lowly deeds of kindness, or in the ways of social influence and homely friendship, we seek to recall all people to their true center, to win them from the world and mammon and self to God.

But we soon find that our good is not strong enough to overcome the evil around us. We meet with misunderstanding and opposition, and our love is too feeble to remain patient and sweet. The warmth kindled by our apostolic zeal cannot survive the impact of another's coldness and disdain, and we find it impossible not to dislike those who seem bent upon making themselves disagreeable. Or, if our love does not succumb to our natural distaste, it surrenders to our craze for popularity. We trim our message, and modify our counsel, and deflect our actions for the sake of winning favor, instead of enduring unpopularity that we may win souls. Or, again, we are tempted to secure a cheap emotional effect, to be content with surface impressions, to suppress troublesome points and evade difficult issues.

If we are sufficiently honest to face facts, we gradually realize that, far from our winning those to whom we are sent, they have mastered us. Almost imperceptibly we have come to regard them from a purely personal point of view, and not in their relation to God and his Kingdom. Their treatment of us has become the most important thing in our eyes, and where that treatment has been harsh, we see ourselves in the center of the picture as martyrs and heroes.

Gradually the sense of our "wrongs" grows upon us, and our happiness comes to depend more and more upon the way in which people receive us. We have, indeed, become the servants of others, but not as St. Paul—for Christ's sake. Our peace of mind hangs upon another's nod. If a sermon or speech or conversational remark of ours meets with cordial response, we are aglow with a sense of apostolic efficiency; but if our utterance is greeted by a frown, and our action interpreted with a sneer, our apostolic confidence melts like snow in the sunshine, and we wonder if we have not pinned our faith to an illusion. That is why the prayerless pulpit is always an uncertain pulpit. The greater part of that recurrent depression and despondency which are supposed to be inseparable from the preacher's temperament is simply the result of a prayerless apostolate, the penalty of looking at people apart from their relation to God.

There comes a moment when we realize that our work for God is a shoddy, futile business, unless it is backed at every point by the apostolate of prayer. We set out full of love, as we thought, and now we find it hard even to tolerate those who oppose us. We thought our apostolic zeal would kindle a fire wherever we went, and now we need all our energy to keep its solitary embers from dying. How are we to recover our first fervor? Not by trying to work ourselves up into a feeling of warmth, but by going back to the prayer of self-oblation, once more offering ourselves to God on behalf of our brethren.

Having done this, our wisdom lies in seeking to understand more deeply and share more fully our Lord's view of those who antagonize and distress us. What do they look like if seen against the background of the cross? How does Christ regard them? It is only as we approach people with his mind concerning them, that our view can be described as apostolic. We must represent not our own view, but the mind of him who sent us, and we can only represent it truly as we become genuinely identified with it "from the inside," as it were, through sustained communion with Christ in his redeeming purpose. It is not a case of putting up with others "for Christ's sake," as conventional religion has it, but of looking at people through Christ's eyes, and seeing in them what he sees in them.

In one of those vivid and, to our modern sense, unpalatably realistic visions of St. Gertrude, we find our Lord showing her his wounded arm wrenched and tortured on the cross, and saying that his arm was being restored whenever she prayed from her heart for certain malicious men who had wrought the monastery grievous harm. "But, Lord," cried St. Gertrude in amazement, "how canst thou call such men thine arm?" The answer came, "I call them so in truth, because they are members of the Body of which I glory to be the Head. Therefore the state of their souls causes me intense anxiety."

Here is a picture, all the more telling because of its naive medieval crudeness, of the Christian conception of human solidarity. The soul that sees people through the magic glass which we call the mind or heart of Christ, sees them not only as members of one another, whereby if one suffers all are affected, but as members of Christ, whose every pulse reverberates in his own heart. The image is worth pondering. If we could really believe that the people who oppose us at every point and make our ministry bitter for us, are to Christ as a bruised and dislocated arm is to a man, how it would change our whole outlook!

And it is "an image of the true." Our foes are not so much alien material that we must somehow transform into stones fit for the temple of God; they are members of the Body to which we belong—crippled and bruised members whose wounds cry for healing. Their sad condition is a challenge to the reality of our own membership in Christ's Body. Without them we cannot be made perfect; without them Christ himself cannot perfect his work of restoration. They are doubly his—as actual members of that humanity which Lacordaire boldly calls "the first church founded by Jesus Christ," and as potential members of that glorious church which is the body of redeemed humanity.

III
A NEW ASSURANCE IN PRAYER

Here is material for profound self-questioning. What is our real motive, our fundamental attitude, in seeking to win other human beings? Are we dominated by a passion for religious and social propaganda or philanthropic activity? That is good as far as it goes, but it falls short of the apostolic ideal. The true apostle goes forth dominated by the sense of his membership with all people in the Body of Christ, and by his consciousness of being sent to heal the wounds in the body of humanity, and the even more tragic wounds in the Body of the Church. He thinks more of the Body than of the repulsive aspect of the sick members. He is animated by the vision of that Body healed and glorious, resplendent in unearthly beauty, and not by any lesser triumph, whether of numbers or influence or any of the other false allurements that beguile the Christian worker.

This may seem high mystical doctrine, but, like so much of what we term "mysticism," it has a most practical import. It faces us with the question as to whether, with all our religious experience and all our strenuous efforts, we are really doing very much to hasten the Kingdom for which Christ lived and died. That Kingdom, as we all admit, is of the spirit. In its upbuilding the motive and attitude of the builder count for everything. A coarse, selfish soul may build a very fine house; but insofar as the House not made with hands is concerned, the person is the work.

If, then, in our work among our fellows, we think much of the slights offered to us, or of the honor accorded to us; if our failures and successes loom large on our horizon; if we attach much importance to the type of person we influence, or to the effect our testimony has upon those we specially admire, we may be builders with God, but it is very doubtful if much of our work will survive the final test. The builder of the Kingdom must have his eye set on the Kingdom, his heart stayed on the King. He must think in terms of the Body. He must bear himself as a member speaking and acting out of the consciousness of that membership, caring little for his own small achievements and reverses, and caring everything for the Body of Christ.

No one will pretend that this attitude is natural to us or that it is easily acquired. It is entirely a product of apostolic prayer, and apostolic prayer is no light undertaking. To beseech blessings for others is comparatively easy, though genuine prayer of any kind is not accomplished without some sweat of soul. But so to offer ourselves to God as to renounce our own thoughts and feelings about our fellows and to accept his instead, brooding upon them until they become woven into our very fiber—that is indeed a task demanding the most heroic qualities. And to this task even the weakest are called, in their own measure. To every Christian soul the divine council-chamber is thrown open. God takes us into his confidence. He wants us to understand and have a share in his decrees of love. He wants apostles, ambassadors who really know his mind, consecrated souls so intimately united to him that they can deal with any situation in his name and in his spirit.

And this opens up a new depth in prayer. If we are to know God's mind, and to know it so intimately as to be able actually to represent it, in our poor human measure, then prayer must involve not merely the outpouring of our souls to God, but also the outpouring of God's heart to us. This seems too startlingly big to be true, but nothing less can equip us for our apostolate. God wants to find a voice, as it were, in the world. He longs to express himself to people. He calls for channels of expression—Christian souls who will continue the work of the Incarnation and be to him as his tongue is to a man. It is free personalities that he desires. He does not want automatic apostleship. He does not use a person as the spiritualist uses mediums. Verbal inspiration has no place in his economy. He calls for living intelligences, for free agents, who shall interpret him out of the abundance of their rich human nature, and do so under no domination or control save that of love.

The term "channel," while almost inevitable, is apt to be misleading in this connection. God's apostles are not passive channels, but active interpreters and exponents of a love that has become their very being. But this implies a reciprocity in prayer. God, as well as humanity, must become vocal. There can be no free appropriation of the divine standpoint, unless God himself explains his longings and opens his heart to the surrendered soul. That he actually does this is a matter of experience. As we become naturalized in the world of prayer, bringing our intellect, as well as our will, to bear upon our communion with God, making our reading and thinking, as well as our daily life, minister to its perfecting, we become conscious of what the mystics have called the "in-speaking" of God in the depth of the soul.

Gently but surely, God reveals himself. Old things gain a new aspect, and the world of humanity is seen in a new light. We know ourselves, and we know God, as we have never done before. Facts of faith become more real and unassailable than facts of sense. We have, as it were, entered the open heart of God, and we are being transformed into its likeness, not by any magic of the religious imagination, but by the sure process of intercommunion, as lover is assimilated to lover and friend to friend.

And gradually we become conscious that as we abide in this state of intercommunion in wholehearted, humble self-surrender, our prayers will be inspired by his overshadowing spirit. Without any loss of freedom, without any sense of psychic mediumship, we shall hear the Lord "pray his prayer within us" and know that the Spirit himself maketh intercession for us. A new sense of calm confidence, a new assurance of victory, will possess us. Realizing with a reverent awe and wonder that we have indeed the mind of Christ, we shall hear him say within our spirits: "Ask what you will, and it shall be done unto you." In the final expression of self-surrender, we shall know our wills—no longer perverse and mistaken, but functioning harmoniously within the will of God—set once more upon the throne. Not bowed in sad submission, but lifted up in humble gladness to the great and glorious Will of God, our wills shall share in the life of apostolic prayer. "Father, *I will*"—it is the will yoked to sacrificial love that speaks. And this wondrous alchemy, which transmutes the dross of self-will into the royal gold of God's will become ours, is wrought in the secret workshop of the soul.

IV

RECOVERING OUR FAITH IN THE CHURCH

To have the will of God, the mind of Christ, concerning ourselves and the world, and to have them not merely by way of intellectual assent or moral appreciation, but by a vital appropriation that assimilates us to our Lord, is to have the key to apostolic power.

Apart from such assimilation, we constantly relapse into a pessimistic view of the prospects of the Kingdom of God upon earth. We see evil triumphant and goodness mocked. We are chilled and disheartened by the mediocrity and feebleness of the good, the compromising weakness of religious men, and the dishonoring timidity of the churches. We see prophets crying in the wilderness, preachers preaching to empty pews, evangelists trying in vain to make the appeal of the gospel more attractive than the appeal of mammon and pleasure. There seems to be a plethora of institutions and workers and an appalling amount of money spent to comparatively little effect. We think we could do with half the churches we have, and more than half of our workers might be better occupied in attending evening classes and working at their own improvement. Day by day the voice of the church, nay, the voice of religion itself, seems to count for less in the popular mind; even regular churchgoers are more influenced by the newspapers than by the message of the pulpit. And so we adduce a formidable volume of evidence to prove that things are in a bad way, and that the church of Christ is dying.

But when we turn from our own interpretation of facts to Christ's vision of the world, we find ourselves breathing in another atmosphere. Whereas we said before, in effect: "The harvest truly is small, and the laborers all too many; that is why they quarrel and wrangle with each other over a handful of ears," Jesus says: "The harvest truly is great, but the laborers are few"; that is why the barns remain empty.

It is our vision that is at fault. No one can reap a harvest he does not see. We look this way and that, and all the time the Lord of the harvest is passing unseen through the field, laden with the sheaves of his prolific passion. We look for our harvest in the people who attend our churches, the money that is contributed to religious objects, the prestige and honor enjoyed by organized religious bodies and their leaders. But Christ looks out upon the world of people. They are his harvest, waiting to be reaped; in them he sees riches enough to fill the treasury of heaven to overflowing. If the church of Christ gave herself to prayer, bent on discovering the mind of her Lord, thirsting to be transformed to his will and purpose; if she said from her heart, *Quo vadis, Domine?* (Where are you going, Lord?), she would surely be led into fields white unto harvest.

Such prayer would make short work of many of our most cherished theories and methods. Matters about which we are almost feverishly concerned would appear as harmless, but quite unimportant, side-issues; modes of work and habits of corporate life to which we are wedded would have to go as so much hampering lumber. We would realize that recognition by the world matters very little, that the only influence of real significance is the influence we have in the secret place of prayer. As the church appears before God, so she really is. If her influence there is negligible, then whatever influence she may seem to wield in the world is so much froth and moonshine.

The true life of the church, as of the individual, is hid with Christ in God. There are times when that life manifests itself in attracting the masses, as it did in the great historical Revivals; but some of the sublimest triumphs of Christ in the world are hidden—hidden often most of all from the workers themselves—and he who is meek and lowly in heart glories in these unseen conquests. Unless, therefore, both the church and the Christian soul are prepared to accept Christ's vision, and to seek first of all and most of all the life and strength that are hidden from the eyes of the world, true success is impossible, and we must content ourselves with a newspaper triumph or a nine-days' religious spasm followed by a dreary reaction.

In apostolic prayer lies the churches' only hope of renewal. Once we learn to pray, individually and corporately, as Christ meant his messengers to pray, the nightmare of an unready world in which preachers and workers have to struggle for spiritual existence will dissolve in the light of day. Instead we will see a world of souls waiting—listening for the footfall of him who preaches the gospel of peace. People who now will not come into our churches, will come into the House of God not made with hands. By what authority were we told to measure the triumph of the Spirit by the number of buildings we can fill? We have the truth of God, we have the good news from God, we have the living Christ. And the world is full of souls who are waiting for what we have to give; it is a matter of going out into the highways and giving our witness bravely and simply.

We need not assume the attitude of shrewd dialecticians, adroit apologists, fervent and feverish persuaders and advocates. "Why so hot, little man?" Before ever the preacher opens his mouth, Christ has already spoken his almighty word in the depth of each soul; before the worker knew his vocation, the Spirit has been at work in the hearts of those to whom he is sent. The Lord always goes before his apostles, and the preacher's best ally is the unseen Witness in the human heart. It is our faithless habit of substituting argument for witness, and criticism for affirmation, that makes so much of our preaching futile. It is our obsession with buildings and institutions that paralyzes us at the critical juncture. Once we grasp firmly that we need not trouble about maintaining anything made of bricks and mortar, that the only thing we have to do is to bring Christ to individual souls, we shall be done with our misgivings and despondency.

This is not meant to belittle the church. On the contrary, we might well ponder the old saying, "Outside the church, no salvation." There *is* a church outside of which there is no salvation—the living Body of Christ. Where that Body is healthy, such matters as buildings and maintenance, the status of the ministry, and the organization of its propaganda, have a way of taking care of themselves. The more strongly we believe in the divine origin and function of the church, the less we will worry about organization and finance. The church, to take the most moderate view, is not only the corporate witness to Christ's presence among humanity, but the organ of that presence. This means that the one thing we need concern ourselves about is *that the church shall really be a church*—holy, catholic, and apostolic; a witness and an organ of Christ on earth, and not a coterie of those who happen to share the same opinions and inherit the same prejudices.

Our anxiety about the institutional aspect of church life and work has its root in a lurking doubt as to the divine authority behind the church. We are not quite sure if the church is but one among many religious institutions destined to serve their purpose and then disappear. To recover our faith in the church and our church consciousness is a crying need of the hour, and we can recover it only through recovering our faith in the living Christ. There is but one way of proving the apostolicity of the church: we must go forth as a church and do the works of the apostles. There is but one way of proving her catholicity: we must bring her treasure to people of all races and nations, types and classes. There is but one way of proving her sanctity: we must demonstrate her power to produce saints in our time.

And there is but one way to such faith—the way of prayer and intercession. Of late we have been much occupied with the respective merits of various forms and types of public worship, and our discovery that many of the old forms and types are outworn has made the whole subject of form and ritual assume a fictitious importance. Aids to prayer and facilities for devotional expression are poor substitutes for the apostolic spirit of prayer, and it is the spirit that is lacking. Once a church is moved to pray, it will pray, no matter how obsolete or inadequate its forms of worship. Its members will meet for prayer, and the spirit of apostolic intercession will master all obstacles and break through all barriers, until each worshiper, as it were, prays "into the hands" of his fellow-worshipers, and the individual's contribution enriches the corporate volume of prayer.

To attain this ideal, we need only begin as individual members of the Body here and now. Where a single apostolic soul gives itself to God in prayer on behalf of Christ's Body, there is the holy catholic church; and the generous, persevering, believing prayer of such a soul can kindle a fire of devotion that will set all Christendom aflame. Only faith is needed: the faith that defies conventions, treads despondency under foot, is prepared to pray a whole lifetime without seeing any visible results, and works from beginning to end by love. Such faith is God's gift to all who dedicate themselves wholeheartedly to the apostolate of prayer.

> He made us to be a kingdom, to be priests unto his God and Father.
>
> *Revelation 1:6 (R.V.)*

> The prophet can preach and witness and pray. He can stimulate, rouse and encourage. But human life needs more than that. It needs the sense of sin forgiven, it needs the life of the incarnate Son, and above all, it needs the assurance that God is in it and with it, and is carrying forward a great and continuous work. It needs a sense of mystery which may stir its depths, a consciousness of things beyond, infinitely greater than it apprehends, a secret feeling of wonder that is ever urging it forward. . . . Priesthood means all these things.
>
> *Bishop Walpole*

CHAPTER SEVEN

The Priesthood of Prayer

WE RECOGNIZE AS NEVER BEFORE that humanity is a circle which needs but to be touched at one point for a vibration to run through the whole. An individual's wisdom or folly, success or failure, do not end with him, any more than they began with him. We owe the practical wisdom, the instructive and almost automatic efficiency, with which we meet everyday requirements to the long and laborious practice of those who went before us. And, equally true, if less obvious, we owe much of our success or failure in meeting new and unexpected demands to the atmosphere created by ourselves, our immediate circle, our community, and our age. To realize this is to discover that life is a responsibility which might well crush us, were it not for the strength and glory that are hidden in the burden of our corporateness. While it may well disquiet us to think that our failure to conquer temptation may involve the failure of our neighbor, it should also inspire us with new courage and hope to remember that we are not alone in our warfare, that the good person by our side is actually helping us.

I

Apostolate and Priesthood

It is for the purpose of belittling the inherent nobility of the great human society, but so that we may rightly interpret and fully actualize it, that we give ourselves to the priesthood of prayer as members of that divine society upon which all human society depends—the Body of Christ. If we have truly entered into the apostolate of prayer, we shall have proved the reality of human solidarity. We shall have realized how mightily the goodness of one single soul, however poor and obscure, can prevail against a host of evil; how literally the spiritual abundance of one can suffice for the sustenance of many; how plain and straight is the path that leads from heart to heart, and through all hearts to the heart of God.

And if we have been true to our apostolate, then sooner or later the priestly heart will be formed in us, and we shall long to enter upon a ministry that apostleship by itself cannot exercise. As we fulfil our divine commission, however, we shall see how even the most humbly surrendered apostle is conscious at times of an impassable barrier between himself and those for whom he prays. Even where that barrier is transcended in the act of prayer, it seems to reappear in our intercourse with our brethren. The reason is not difficult to find: it is that our personality, with all its limitations and flaws, prejudices and repugnancies, comes between us and our neighbor, obstructing the divine influence that is waiting to work through us. Sometimes it is our peculiarities and angularities that stand in the way; at other times it is our excellences—the very qualities in us that attract and charm—that constitute the barrier. And recognizing that our work is hindered, we are tempted to wish this troublesome gift of personality away.

It is not, however, the fact of personality that is the obstacle. A strong and attractive personality is always a most valuable apostolic asset. But there are times when personality must recede, occasions when the prophet must give way to the priest, if the work of God is to be done. Until we have learned the art of priestly self-effacement, we shall not be able to make full use of our apostolic personality. So far from being incompatible functions, the apostolic and the priestly activities are complementary elements of our divine calling. Some are doubtless called to exemplify the priestly aspect in a special way, and others to magnify the apostolic function, but this does not contradict the fundamental truth that both apostolate and priesthood are common to all believers.

There is, however, an important distinction between the two aspects. The apostolate may be exercised upon purely individual lines, and history has shown that the detached apostle, whose freelance activity may cause grave misgivings to rigid ecclesiastics, has a great and unique function to perform in the building up of the Kingdom of God. But it is different in the case of the priesthood. While the detached believer who offers himself to God on behalf of humanity is doubtless a true priest of humanity, the full Christian priesthood of believers is conditional upon their participation in the priestly life of the whole Body of Christ. It follows that the main reason why our sense of priesthood is so weak today, notably among Free Churchmen, is that we have lost that corporate consciousness which springs from a worthy doctrine of the one church.

There is a general dissatisfaction among earnest Christians with the poverty of our public worship and the feebleness of our private devotions, but comparatively few realize that the fundamental cause of this decline is that we have largely lost the doctrine of the one church. It is hardly necessary to say that this doctrine may be held in a dead, superstitious manner, and that it always will be so held where it is not derived from and subordinated to the doctrine of the living Christ. But given true faith in the living Christ, it is the lack of a true conception of the church catholic and holy, and of our relationship to her, that accounts for our present-day bankruptcy of devotional life. One can see no prospect of a genuine revival of worship apart from a revival of the apostolic doctrine of the church.

All true lovers of Christ rejoiced in the Lambeth Proposals of 1920. Churchmen of the most widely different views agreed that these Resolutions were born of a wonderful vision of Christian unity, and reflected a spirit of deep penitence and love; most people have seen in the definiteness of the proposals an additional proof of the genuineness of the feeling that prompted them. But this very definiteness has tended to make us look upon their scope in much too narrow a way. We are in danger of defeating their object and frustrating their spiritual influence by viewing them almost exclusively as a definite scheme for promoting the union of two relatively small sections of the church of Christ within the British Empire. Such a union, it is clear, cannot restore to us that apostolic sense of a worldwide Christian fellowship which alone can make the priesthood of believers a living fact.

There is only one ideal that can produce a universal and immutable sense of the solidarity of humanity and of the priestly office of Christians towards their brethren, and that is the ideal of a world-wide universal church. The Lambeth Proposals, while themselves inspired by that ideal, have ironically made it more difficult for many to gain a clear and commanding vision of the one church. The resolutions call on us to start from the denomination we happen to be in, and to consider how that denomination can find its place as one corporate group among many in a larger church, without surrender of principle or stultification of its particular ministry. We speak of the genius, mind, witness, and mission of "our" church, and we express our willingness to confer with the representatives of other religious bodies, to see how that genius, mind, witness, and mission can be conserved and rendered effective in union with "other people's churches." From such an attitude no truly united church can ever come.

Our only salvation lies in forgetting our separate bodies, insofar as they are separate, and praying for a new vision of the church catholic, the only church to whose mind and witness we owe our loyalty. That church does not stop at the gates of Rome, or exclude the ancient communions of the East, nor is it exhausted by any or all of the existing ecclesiastical bodies. It includes a great body of lovers of Jesus Christ who, through ignorance or prejudice, have not sought admission into the visible church, even though they are as real and as important a part of it as the most highly organized and fully doctrinal section. Christian consciousness will never rest in any conception short of one that includes all who love the Lord Jesus Christ in sincerity, while giving their due value to ecclesiastical tradition and order.

II
THE DIVINE SOCIETY

If this church is indeed God's will for us, how can we realize it? What force can bring Rome, Orthodoxy, Anglicanism, and Nonconformity into one Christian fellowship? Such union presupposes a radical change, and the great obstacle in the way of such a change lies not in the realm of ecclesiastical conviction, but in a region where we rarely think of looking for it—in our evil heart of unbelief.

Whatever we may hold in theory, in practice we still draw a sharp line between the individual and the community. We believe in individual repentance and conversion; we do not really believe that churches and whole nations can repent and be changed.

And even when we are convinced by the testimony of history that nations as well as human beings can be born in one day, and that a dead church can rise at the bidding of Christ as truly as a dead soul, we persist in imagining that the work of corporate regeneration is of a quasi-occult nature, practically independent of human cooperation. We pray with fervor for the redemption of a prodigal son, but the moment it is a question of a prodigal nation, our prayers become conventional and lifeless. When it is a prodigal church that is in question, we are sorely tempted to cease from prayer and, turning our backs upon that church, to seek salvation in individualistic ways.

The truth is that God is waiting for our prayers so that he might heal the wounds of the church. If the Body of Christ remains weakened and dismembered, it is because we have not risen to our calling to cooperate with him in its restoration. We ask how this cooperation is to be effected, how any kind of effort towards true union can have its legitimate result, so long as we cannot agree upon a basis for such effort. We see no way out of the tangle, and we finally turn from the unprofitable disputes of rival sects and parties to the Christ who stands above them all, and who has the words of eternal life for each soul. Whatever else may be true, this is indubitably certain: that in Christ there is newness of life for every person and that we need not wait for church councils and inter-church conferences before taking up the cross and following him.

We are fundamentally social beings, and our hearts crave

for fellowship in the Christian faith. Nor can we study the origins of Christianity without recognizing that Christ as well as the Apostles conceived of Christian discipleship as a divine society. Moreover, our own experience bears witness to our need of a fullness of life that can only come to us as members of a corporate body. Individual discipleship, even if it is of the highest quality, must remain one-sided and in danger of eccentricity or fanaticism, unless it brings its contribution to the corporate fellowship and draws from that fellowship what it needs to supply its lack.

No matter where we start, sooner or later we shall be driven back upon the church of Christ. We see the church split up into proud and ambitious factions; we see her debased by dishonoring alliances with the world and the spirit of the time. And yet, tempted as we may be to turn our backs upon her, relegating her to the realm of outworn institutions, we are held back by the thought that God would not have given us so exacting a conception of what the church ought to be, if he had not ordained that she can and still will become all we envision her to be, and more. And if that is his will, it is up to us to consider how we can help to bring it to pass.

The whole subject is hedged about by a prickly fence of controversy, but in the ultimate resort the way out of the tangle is a simple one. We need only go back to the individual, and ask ourselves what is the best way to cooperate with God in seeking the good of some soul we love. Whatever may be our way with that soul must be our way with the church; any less personal and more ambitious method is pure delusion.

It has been the aim of this study to show how the essence of prayer is the soul's self-donation and how in intercessory prayer that self-donation is made on behalf of others. To pray for the conversion of a soul means to dedicate oneself to God on behalf of that soul, and at its highest point such prayer assumes a priestly character. We no longer assert our personality, either by way of persuasion towards that individual, or by way of impassioned pleading towards God. Such assertion of personality has its place in prayer, but there are levels of communion with God—and those the highest levels—at which it yields to a sense of priesthood, and the consecrated soul becomes a vehicle of grace. It becomes at once priest and sacrifice, filling up that which is lacking of the sufferings of Christ on behalf of others. In such prayer we lose ourselves, and so enter both into the misery and want of those for whom we offer ourselves and into the redemptive sufferings of Christ, sharing with him in his saving work.

The objection that such sharing in the work of redemption detracts from the uniqueness of Christ's atoning work is no more valid in this case than it would be if our pain and penitence for our own sins and failings were in question. If our personal repentance and sorrow do not impair the finished work of Christ, why should the pain and sorrow we offer him on behalf of others be derogatory to his unique Saviorhood? Whatever may be our theory, the moment we grasp the meaning of prayer as creative energy, our practice will be that of priestly intercession and sacrifice.

III

PRIESTLY PRAYER: SERVING THE ALTAR

Such priestly intercession means self-denying effort. To say that no one can repent for another is true, if we mean thereby that no one can be saved without repenting for himself. But if we mean to deny that our penitence for the sins of another may be the most effectual means of inducing that other person to repent for himself, we have not yet learned the elementary meaning of human solidarity.

There is nothing artificial in such vicarious penitence. The sins of others do affect and involve us, whether we like it or not. As a matter of hard fact, we already have a share in them. They are a part of the sin-laden atmosphere that makes goodness so difficult for us, as for all people; they are part of the tragic reason why we find it so hard to keep the lamp of faith burning, and why the music of our hope is so often drawn from a single slender string. Our sins are certainly our own, as our neighbor's sins are not, but the effect of our neighbor's sins—his shame and misery, his pain and remorse, or, more tragic still, his indifference, pride, and levity, which bring an even deeper pain to the Father's heart than the sins themselves—this surely must concern and affect us in a very real and weighty sense.

The moment we turn away from the narrower vision, which sees in our neighbor's sins a lowering of the general moral temperature and a decline in the general moral health of humanity, to the larger vision, which sees them as God sees them, then we begin to long to atone for them as Christ atones, and priestly prayer becomes as natural as the air we breathe. We no longer stop short at pleading with God on behalf of the sinner; nothing short of bearing his burden and letting his shame and pain fall on us will suffice for our awakened conscience. We have the faith of our Lord Jesus Christ—not merely faith in him, but the same faith that he had. Since his faith led him to offer himself, body, soul, and spirit, as a sacrifice for sin, our faith compels us to enter into communion with him in that sacrifice—not, indeed, because we can atone for either ourselves or our brethren, but because we know he can and we are one with him.

Such priestly prayer demands the highest form of courage and fortitude. When we offer ourselves to God on behalf of a sinner, we do not know to what length and intensity of painful effort we are pledging ourselves; we only know that in the case of our great High Priest it meant a sacrifice that covered his whole life and culminated in death.

If we would be true priests of intercession, we must be ready and willing to "serve the altar," for a lifetime if need be, without seeing any result. We must have the implicit faith, the unquenchable hope, the all-enduring love that is willing to continue praying in union with the eternal intercession of the ascended Lord, even though the world sneers and the church looks askance at us, and those for whom we pray seem to grow worse rather than better. We must be content to garner no harvest, to gain no recognition. We must find in the misery of those who have turned from God, and most of all in the misery of those who are happy in their alienation from God, ceaseless fuel for the altar fire. Through union with Christ our love must gain a quality of substitutionary sympathy which never becomes exhausted or dulled by self-regard.

This can be achieved only through a growing union with Christ. Natural human sympathy soon wears thin, and the first glow of apostolic fervor is chilled; but union with Christ in his sacrificial priesthood turns what seems to the uninitiated to be an intolerable burden into a labor of love and a source of the purest joy. Creative prayer is like a temple. To enter the outer court is not so difficult, and to stand in the holy place is always possible to devout souls; but the Holy of Holies is a place of priestly sacrifice, and many truly earnest souls shrink from its exacting demands and seek to persuade themselves that the altar is not everyone's vocation. But in the temple of prayer, as in every temple, it is the altar that sanctifies and interprets the whole, and only those who serve the altar have really grasped the secret of communion with God.

Exalt joy as we may—and there is surely no joy to be compared to that of the Christian adventure—it is not to the pilgrim in quest of joy that the secret of the Lord is revealed, but to the lover of the cross, bent on sacrifice.

It is because so many enter the holy ministry with thoughts other than that of "self-sacrifice to the mystery of redemption," and because so many give themselves to Christian work or to prayer unsustained by that master-motive, that their ministry remains ineffectual and they grow weary in well-doing. If there is one thing above any other that we need to preach to ourselves and our age, it is that there is nothing fruitful except sacrifice; that Christ has once and for all "shown mankind that when God would save the world, even he could only die for it."

The model of our priesthood, and he who alone can form the priestly heart in us, is Jesus Christ himself. He conquered the world by giving himself for it, and so must we. If we want our prayers to bear fruit through all the circles of spiritual existence, we must join them to his high priestly prayer. We may, if we will, become cooperators with him and through him obtain gifts for our brethren. It lies in our power to hasten or to retard the final restoration of all things in him. The one condition of our cooperation with him in the work of redemption is that we should, like him, efface self and, with him, offer ourselves up to the Father as instruments of his grace towards humanity. "My food," said Jesus, "is to do the will of him who sent me . . ." (John 4:34). "By myself I can do nothing; I judge only as I hear, and my judgment is just: for I seek not to please myself but him who sent me" (John 5:30). "My teaching is not my own; it comes from him who sent me" (John 7:16).

When our Lord responded to the disciples' request to be taught how to pray, he began by drawing their thoughts away from himself and teaching them to say, "Our Father." And when it became clear to him that this priestly surrender meant obedience unto death, even death on the cross, he still did not take back the self he had so royally surrendered, but gave his body to the smiters and his soul to the agony of Love's struggle with sin. And to each of us, with hearts divided between our love to him and our natural shrinking from pain, he says, *"As the Father hath sent me, even so send I you."*

Only the consciousness of being thus sent will arm us with that "sweet, long patience" which is requisite for priestly prayer. Only the strength of his cross will enable us to bow our souls beneath the burden of sin not our own and to allow our hearts to be pierced with his pain. Nor does this priestly prayer consist merely in one heroic act, or even in a succession of such acts. It involves a life habit; it means that in everything that comes to us of joy or sorrow, temptation or victory, we shall see an opportunity for the exercise of our priesthood.

When it goes hard with us in the spiritual combat, we shall resist the inclination to think of ourselves, but instead make our temptations an opportunity to pray for all who are tempted in the same way, asking that our victory may make it easier for them also to conquer. When sorrow falls upon us, we shall put the temptation to self-pity beneath our feet and offer ourselves and our grief to God on behalf of those who sorrow uncomforted and know not how to turn their distress into enlargement of soul. When joy comes to us, we shall seek so to welcome and use it as to be the priest of all who laugh and are glad, that they may keep their joy pure and that it may become their strength.

Priestly prayer means a selfless life. And yet the priestly instinct is the human instinct. It is the same impulse as that which leads the mother to live for her child, impels the patriot to consecrate all he has and is to his country, and enables friend to die for friend. Grace is supernatural, not unnatural, and the grace of priesthood is as germane to God's children, and as freely bestowed upon all who desire it, as is mother-love and patriotic passion.

IV

HEALING THE CHURCH'S WOUNDS

We are now in a position to see how this priestly prayer operates in the sphere of corporate life and how it is the very sustenance of the Body of Christ. In praying for individuals, the first need is the vision of faith. We must see the people we pray for as restored in Christ. However stained and covered with shame they be, we must see them transmuted into loveliness, made pure and glorious, triumphing over their foes and reaching their high destiny. We must believe in their capacity for repentance, their possibility of renewal, their hidden virtues, their unseen aspirations. And our faith in Christ's redeeming love must be so strong and unshakable that we shall be ready to give our whole life to intercession, and still believe and hope, even though the day of our death finds those souls unchanged.

And in thinking of the corporate body we must strive after the same faith. We must see, not the torn, stained church of actuality, but the church glorious, without spot or wrinkle or any such thing; and we must ground our vision not on poetic fancy, but on the promise of him who loved the Bride and gave himself for her. We must hold this faith though faced with the obvious unloveliness and the crying scandal of a divided and dismembered church. We must have faith to believe that the most intolerant, the most superstitious, the most pharisaical sections of the church can be purged and transformed, can melt into repentance, can glow with evangelic fervor, and can thrill with a desire for true unity in Christ Jesus. We must believe that even now the redemption of the church is at hand; that the Lord stands at the door, waiting only for us to share his priestly work, hindered only by our reluctance to watch and agonize, to believe and hope, with him.

Whatever may be our ecclesiastical inheritance and its justification, it must be laid upon the altar of our priesthood to be purified and purged of self-will, lest it obscure our vision and hinder our faith in the one church as it exists in the mind of Christ. At the bottom of our unwillingness to unite with those of other communions lies a radical want of faith. We are enamored of the fragment of truth that our own communion represents. We believe it to be indeed divine. And yet we do not sufficiently trust him who committed it to us, to run the risk involved in bringing it to the common stock of the church catholic. We do not realize that three-fourths of what we mistake for loyalty to principle, is sheer lack of faith in the church's Lord. The church remains dismembered because her rival sections have not yet learned that he who seeks to save his life shall lose it. All are struggling furiously for existence; none is willing to die unto itself that it may find its true life in the life of the whole Body.

And so we remain bound in sectarianism, frightened of the intolerance—or laxity, as the case may be—of sister denominations, too timid and ungenerous to trust the vision of a church penitent, enlightened, and gloriously restored. Our vision of the one church is, indeed, too dim to grip us in the face of the unlovely reality of warring fragments, too dim to make us realize our membership in the undivided Body and its claim upon our loyalty.

Some of our leaders lament the decrease of denominational loyalty and the growing tendency to avoid church attendance altogether. But no loyalty short of loyalty to the one church is of ultimate importance; at best, sectional loyalty is only a higher species of club consciousness. It is one of the gravest symptoms of our spiritual disorder that the average Christian has come to regard the church as little more than "the social expression of a certain predetermined unanimity of opinion among the individuals who compose it." We join a particular section of the church because we believe certain things, i.e., hold certain religious opinions. When we change those opinions, or when, in our judgment, the section we have joined ceases to express them or to interpret them rightly, we disassociate ourselves from it—"resign our membership" (to use the ominous phrase borrowed from club terminology), thereby unconsciously revealing the degradation to which the popular conception of churchmanship has sunk.

But if, in lieu of such club loyalty, the spirit of loyalty to the Body of Christ were to be poured out upon Christendom; if we realized afresh that the church was not of our making, but of his—that far from our having the right to make irresponsible demands upon her, she has a divine claim upon our loyalty, and demands that we should bring all our gifts and ministries, priestly and prophetic, to her treasury—the day of true church union would not be far off.

This does not mean that the church is above criticism. We not only may, we *must* judge her, but we must judge her according to her inherent laws, and not according to our individual opinions. Catholicity, apostolicity, sanctity—these are her infallible marks. If she is not catholic, apostolic, and holy, it is our responsibility to discern it, but only that we may strive to make her so once more.

If she is not catholic today, will our mutual distrust, or the timid, prudential compromises which we miscall union, help to make her so? If she is not apostolic, will our mammon-worship, our cheap, popular pulpit, our worldly methods, our ecclesiastical scheming restore her to apostolic dignity and power? If she is not holy, will our jealousies and rivalries, our zest for scandal, and our dishonorable exposing of her faults to the public gaze wash her robes and make them white? We pride ourselves upon our freedom from ecclesiastical tyranny; we boast of our enlightened private judgment in criticizing and carping at the church. It is the freedom, if we like to call it such, of the man who publishes his mother's shame in the marketplace! It is the denial of Christ's own vision, the frustration of his hopes, the stultification of his high priestly prayer. It is the sin against the ideal of the divine society; it is the grieving of the Spirit by whom we are called.

But if those of us who have seen the vision splendid of the one church and who have heard her Lord's voice bidding us heal her wounds, would from henceforth give ourselves in priestly prayer for her healing, a new era would surely dawn. Our noblest workers are discouraged, our most impassioned apostles seem impotent, because they are trying to do as individuals those "greater works" which only the corporate body, restored and transfigured, can do in their fullness. There is only one way to repair the House of God, to redeem the Bride of Christ—the self-oblation of priestly souls, brave enough, believing enough, patient enough to give themselves to prayer for the church without seeing any visible results, and, in an atmosphere of division and disaffection, to live as members of the one Body.

V

SEEING SINNERS AS FORGIVEN

We have based our study of creative prayer upon the assumption that the value of prayer depends in every case upon the life behind it, and still more upon the life which it produces. There can be no truly apostolic prayer without the development of apostolic personality, and there can be no offering of priestly intercession without the formation of the priestly character.

But what constitutes the priestly character? In reality, the Christian priesthood is not a hierarchic caste, but a representative class. The priest's significance is corporate. He acts for the whole body; far from detracting from the priesthood of all believers, he gives it the fullest expression, uniting it with the priesthood of Christ himself. And whatever view we may take on the subject of the ordained priesthood, a very little thought will convince us that the priesthood of all believers must belong to the same order. It can mean no less than the mediation of that remission and washing away of sins which is symbolized by the sacrament of baptism, and the mediation of the divine communication of new life which is symbolized by the sacrament of Holy Communion. No opinion of the nature of ordination can dispense us from the obligation of realizing our own priestly function as members of Christ's Body; we are to magnify the priestly calling which is common to us all. The question of Orders is quite irrelevant to the matter; the only question that concerns us is how we, who live in the world and are engaged in ordinary secular work, can fulfil our priesthood.

The task before us is clear. We are faced by a world of people bound and weighed down by sin. In some, sin appears as open rebellion against all that is good and noble; in others it can be discerned only by the spiritual expert as one of those subtle and almost impalpable forms of self-love which so often robe themselves in a cloak of altruism. Sin, like all evil, can take a very high polish and appear as extremely pleasing to the untutored eye; but once the black thread in the web of life is discerned, it is easy to trace it to the darkness whence it came.

And as we go about among others with unsealed eyes, we come to realize more and more that their supreme need is to become conscious of their sin. Not defiance but self-deception is the most fatal and widespread disease of the human heart. People live and die in sin, not because they consciously rebel against God, but because they do not know that there is anything very seriously wrong in their relation to their Maker. They are guilty of self-righteousness—the one attitude that seems to defy the grace of God—not because they put their trust in external observances, but because they cannot see any reason for trying to achieve a "righteousness"—whether that of the Pharisees, or that which exceeds it—other than the goodness they imagine themselves to possess without trying. Their eyes are blinded, their sense of need is unawakened, and they remain estranged from God and cut off from their true life.

Over against them stands the great Lover of souls, with forgiveness, cleansing, newness of life in his hands; between them and him stand we who have been forgiven and know the secret of new life through union with Christ. How can we, priests of divine mysteries, mediate forgiveness to those who do not see the need of being forgiven, healing to those who deem themselves whole, life from the dead to those who think themselves triumphantly alive?

The conventional answer is that they must first, by preaching and teaching, be roused to a sense of need. The evangelist must stir their sluggish emotions, the apostle must recall their wayward wills, the teacher must enlighten their dull minds. Moreover, before the forgiveness of God can come to them, they must not only be convinced of sin, but also be melted to penitence. There must be confession—clear, definite, full, contrite; and if their spiritual guide be one who believes in the "sacrament of penance," he will urge the salutary effect of confessing to a priest, if, indeed, he does not insist upon it as a necessity. The priest, he will remind them, acts as the representative of the Family of God. He discharges a corporate function. And since his absolution is valid only if the penitent has made a full, honest, and truly contrite confession, the "sacrament of penance," far from being strictly a priestly imposition, is practically self-administered.

However, this whole conception of a forgiveness that is contingent upon contrition and repentance cuts clean across the fundamental principle of the gospel. This is one of those modifications of the Christian message to which both lay and ecclesiastical human nature is peculiarly prone. It is a plausible way of reducing Christianity from a gospel to a contract, and of taking the supernatural out of the very act of God. It is the favorite refuge of timid and faithless souls, the working axiom of those who want to look before they leap. Its rehabilitation among earnest people has a far closer connection than we think with that postwar decline of religion which certain optimistic prophets found so bitterly disillusioning, for it touches the very source and mainspring of all spiritual endeavor.

What is the Christian message? Is it a refined version of the moral code which "all good men," including heathens and publicans, obey, or is it a new life whose morality begins where that of the natural human being leaves off? Is it the sweetness and light that transfigures natural religion, or is it the revelation of God that challenges it? Unless we are ourselves convinced, and can impress others with the conviction that Christianity is not merely a moral code, however elevated and beneficent, but a gospel of free, unmerited forgiveness, and that to be a Christian means to make that gospel the charter of our life, we have little to be very enthusiastic about.

Edifices of morality, and especially of natural morality superficially Christianized, spring up in every age, and it takes no crusade to secure builders; but the New Jerusalem of the forgiven and cleansed life comes down from heaven, and they who look for it must be prepared to be accounted fools and to bear their witness without waiting for a response.

The forgiveness that lies at the heart of the Christian gospel, of which we are priests, is something other than the absolution pronounced upon the penitent—an absolution entirely right in its own place—by an official representative of the redeemed Family against which he has sinned. It is rather the forgiveness of the Son of Man, who said to the paralytic before he had uttered a single word of confession, "Son, be of good cheer; your sins are forgiven you"; the forgiveness of the Crucified, who prayed concerning his impenitent and brutal executioners, "Father, forgive them, for they know not what they do." Far from being "self-administered," it is a stupendous, creative act of God—the "divine indiscretion" and redemptive paradox that constitute the originality of the Christian gospel. Its daring, revolutionary challenge and its sublime adventure lie here.

To look upon sinners, seeing their obvious impenitence, sensing the hideous twist in their natures, recognizing their weakness and brokenness of will, knowing the detestable tendency of crass human nature to mistake gentleness for weakness and make mercy an excuse for sin—to discern all this, and *still* to assure them of God's free, full forgiveness, trusting both him and them where appearances are dead against such trust, is the great Christian adventure. To turn our backs upon the prudential counsels of those who would see repentance before they speak of forgiveness, and to side with him who commended his love towards us in that while we were yet sinners, Christ died for us, is to accept and fulfill our priestly vocation. It takes courage and faith such as can be learned only from our great Brother-Priest. It takes long endurance, implicit obedience to the heavenly vision, steadfast perseverance in face of criticism, disappointment, and estrangement; but it is the only path that leads to the altar-throne.

It is becoming more and more the fashion to minimize the constructive doctrinal achievement of the leaders of the Reformation, and to reduce their work to a barren protest against ecclesiastical tyranny; to insist, indeed, that the freedom they stood for was nothing more important than freedom from the authority of the Bishop of Rome. Nothing could be more shallow than such an estimate. Argue as we may, there is not only in the message of St. Paul, but also in the life and words of our Lord himself, a principle of free grace, a law of justifying faith, which traditional theology had obscured and traditional ecclesiastical practice had rendered of none effect. It was the rediscovery of the divine law of forgiveness that gave the Reformation its liberating force. In the Reformers the Christian consciousness reverted to its creative principle; the soul of the church became aware of the laws of its being. In them the Evangelical instinct, which had never died out of the church, became articulate and found intellectual justification.

The cleavage between mystical and institutional religion, on the one hand, and between what may be called the faith type and the penance type, on the other, did not come into being with the Reformation. It always existed both in Rome and in the Orthodox churches of the East, but in Luther and Calvin its theological basis and intellectual implications were laid bare. Existing up till then as an unformulated tendency, the Pauline element in the church's theology became at the

Reformation a doctrinal system, producing a distinct spiritual attitude and outlook. We may criticize that system as we will—it is obviously one-sided, and suffers from having been worked out in an atmosphere of reaction and revolt—but the very isolation and over-emphasis with which the Reformers presented it served to recall an enslaved Christian consciousness to the freedom wherewith Christ had made it free, as a more harmoniously balanced presentation could not have done.

The Reformers displayed before the eyes of Christendom its charter of liberty in six-foot letters, as it were, of the boldest type. And the type was not an atom too bold for the occasion. "The gospel, which is our warrant of acquittal, has not yet been read by all," said Chateaubriand a hundred years ago, and it still holds true today. For the majority of professing Christians, the gospel is still a strange tale, heard as in a dream and only half believed, if believed at all. And until the proclamation of Christian liberty has been "read by all," the Reformation, far from being superseded, is of prophetic significance, and its hour is yet to come.

And if we, seeking to realize our priestly vocation, will dare to take our stand boldly upon this divine "warrant of acquittal," we shall know what it is that our Lord has committed to us. The power to loose individuals from their sins, or to bind them in their sins, will become an everyday reality. As we refuse to associate the sinner with his sin, but persist in seeing him as forgiven, and have the faith to treat him as forgiven, the fetters of sin shall drop off him, and the new man shall arise out of the ruins of the old. This does not mean to juggle with the reality of sin. "Thou art Simon," said our Lord; there was no attempt to ignore the imperfect present. "Thou shalt be called Cephas"; there was no attempt to weaken the message of hope for fear of encouraging a presumptuous or careless temper. "If only we had that radiant insight, that prophetic vision!" we say. Rather, if only we could see the glorious possibility!

But the fault lies elsewhere than merely in a lack of vision. If we had the priestly heart, the priestly passion to mediate God's forgiveness to our brethren at the cost of whatever sacrifice, the vision would come of itself. Then, instead of binding men in their sins by our refusing to see them as Christ sees them, their chains would snap at our coming. Then the simple word of encouragement, spoken with prayer behind it, would reverberate through eternity, as the absolution of the Great High Priest ratified our proclamation of faith.

VI

The Essence of Discipleship

From first to last, the priesthood of Jesus meant personal sympathy, and personal sympathy that extended to the homeliest details and rose to sacrificial passion. He began his priestly life by an act of identification with his sinful brethren in his baptism in the Jordan. There he deliberately laid himself alongside penitent humanity. He went down into the sacramental flood for those who wept in penitence and for those who refused to repent for themselves. And this ministry of identification was the very stuff of his life on earth. No one can read the Gospels without sensing the intensity and tenderness of sympathy that runs through them, expressed and unexpressed. When he proclaimed the children's charter, he took the little ones into his arms. When he sent the rich young ruler away sorrowful, it was with deep personal affection in his eyes. When he instituted the Holy Supper, his favorite disciple leaned on his breast.

The reason our intercession is so poor and intermittent, depending upon an effort of faith to which we are often quite inadequate, is that we do not realize that it is, in truth, our divine vocation. Priesthood is the essence of Christian discipleship. As we are called to follow our Lord in our daily life and our apostolic work, so we are called to tread in his footsteps in the way of priesthood. We are not sent to the altar on our own charges; he who called us is responsible for our maintenance. He is ready to impart to us his faith in humanity, his unquenchable hope, his unfailing love. Provided we are willing to dedicate ourselves wholeheartedly to the life of priestly intercession, asking to see no results, and are prepared, as opportunity arises, to substantiate our prayers by the word of forgiveness, hope, and cheer, and still more by the self-giving love that speaks louder than words, then we shall find it true that he who serves the altar shall live by the altar.

Much is involved here, for our priesthood, like our apostolate, is world-wide. It pledges us to purge ourselves of a narrowing national consciousness and to put ourselves under the burden of the groaning peoples of the earth. It involves our emptying ourselves of all class-feeling and taking into our very heart the needs and claims of the class with which we have the least natural sympathy; and very often that will be not the oppressed, but the dominant and domineering class. If we search ourselves we may come to see that the reason we cry in vain, "When wilt thou save the people?" is that while we are overflowing with sympathy for the downtrodden masses, whose misery disarms our prejudice, we are filled with resentment against some section of our own class that happens to oppose our views, or of the class above us against whose insolence our sympathy is not immune.

When shall we realize that we cannot be effectual intercessors for any individual or any body of people until we have learned to be priests of humanity? As long as we let our indignation, however justifiable that indignation may be, betray us into partisanship, our prayers shall beat the air. In approaching people our one thought must be, not how they may be made more conformable to our tastes and ideas, but how we can most fully enter into their point of view, voice their needs, and give expression to their uninformed and often unconscious aspirations.

This brings us to the crown and glory of priestly prayer. We are called to be mediators—to enter into the mind of the Lord and voice his appeal to humanity, and to enter into the heart of humanity and voice its cry to God; to represent both the forgiving love and redeeming passion of Christ and the struggling aspirations and half-choked longings of the souls of human beings. What completeness of self-emptying is needed for such a task, what relentless mortification and unsparing sacrifice!

There is only one way of achieving so high a destiny. We must resolutely resist all temptations to take an easier path than that of personal consecration and personal sympathy, and we must repudiate every theological system that makes more of "the Faith" than of "the faith of our Lord Jesus Christ." The following of Christ in the way of priesthood is a slow and inward process. It means a daily offering of our bodies and spirits. It means being not less human but more so, for the true priest of intercession is one who has been clothed with universal humanity. He has opened his heart to the wants and claims of opposing nations, classes, and parties, and realized within himself, in human measure, the all-inclusive and sacrificial sympathy of his Lord.

And so he stands before the altar mediating forgiveness, radiating newness of life, trusting himself, body and soul, into the hands of his Lord to be broken for the feeding of thousands, to feel within himself the darkness and despair, the bitter longing and struggle of sinning humanity, and the mystery of Christ's dereliction on the cross.

His priesthood, then, is in his love. He is no remote hieratic figure, hidden from his fellows as the priest is hidden within the confessional; he is a shelter from the heat, a covert from the tempest, and as the shadow of a great rock in a weary land. He is a living, throbbing center in which divine grace and human longing meet.